Sunday Morning

ABOUT THE AUTHOR

Michael H. Ducey was born in Chicago. He spent fourteen years (1952-66) in the Jesuit order, the last seven of them in India. He took a B.A. and an M.A. in Philosophy from Xavier University (Cincinnati) and Loyola University (Chicago) in the 50's and then, after his term in India, returned to the University of Chicago, where he received an M.A. and a Ph.D. in Sociology. *Sunday Morning,* the product of his lifelong interest in contemporary religion and urban problems, is an adaptation of his dissertation and is his first book-length publication. Mr. Ducey is currently a participant in the Youth in Illinois Project sponsored by the Institute for Juvenile Research. With Gary Marx, he is at work on a long-range project on youth culture in several settings.

SUNDAY MORNING

Aspects of Urban Ritual

Michael H. Ducey

THE FREE PRESS
A Division of Macmillan Publishing Co., Inc.
NEW YORK
Collier Macmillan Publishers
LONDON

The Free Press
A Division of Macmillan Publishing Co., Inc.
866 Third Avenue, New York, N.Y. 10022

Collier Macmillan Canada, Ltd.

Library of Congress Catalog Card Number: 76-25342

Printed in the United States of America

printing number

1 2 3 4 5 6 7 8 9 10

Library of Congress Cataloging in Publication Data

Ducey, Michael H
   Sunday morning.

   Includes bibliographical references and index.
   1. Chicago--Churches--Case studies. 2. Public
worship--Case studies. 3. Lincoln Park neighborhood,
Chicago. 4. Chicago--Social conditions. I. Title.
BR560.C4D8   301.5'8   76-25342
ISBN 0-02-907640-4

Contents

Acknowledgments

For fourteen years, my numerous Jesuit teachers honed my mind and disciplined my spirit. They also exposed me to a wide range of culture and knowledge. I hope these intellectual gifts plus the Rules for the Discernment of Spirits have become a permanent part of my attempts to understand the world.

I am indebted to many at the University of Chicago. Gerald Suttles introduced me to field work and encouraged me to find my own way. Victor Lidz was a patient listener as I tried to formulate my thoughts. Joseph Kitagawa encouraged and deepened my interest in religion. Victor Turner showed me the value of erudition and of mastery of the traditions of scholarship. We differ in value orientations, but I hope we use the same rational techniques of argument. Morris Janowitz was supportive when support counted. Donald Levine provided crucial aid and stimulation when things looked worst. His intervention saved this work from oblivion. My colleague Gary Schwartz at the Institute for Juvenile Research gave me time, encouragement, and suggestions all along the way.

I am indebted to many people who talked openly with me as I tried to do research on their religion. I am especially grateful to the members of the congregation of the Church of the Three Crosses. Hopefully their contributions to this work will be repaid in some measure by the clarifications offered in this work.

Introduction

Religion will always be a more important phenomenon than the sociology of religion. This is so not because religion is the opiate of the masses and society will always be composed of a mass that needs an opiate; rather it is because religion is the web of symbols that link humankind to the ground of human existence. There are opiative forms of religion and truly liberating forms of religion. A pessimistic view of history says the opiate will always be required. An optimistic view says that eventually the race will institutionalize the best that human nature is capable of. But in both views, religion remains a fundamental institution of human society.

The sociology of religion has at best a midwife role in the construction of religious systems. The criticism of religion at *its* best is a dialectical negation of obsolete forms of consciousness. At its worst it is a petulant reaction to symbolic oppression which ends by changing the form of oppression, not transcending it. One takes an active part in the ground of human existence through contemplation and belief. One takes a progressive part in the history of human existence through art, thought, and self-critical action. What I understand by the sociology of religion is the thoughtful complement to contemplation and belief.

The pages which follow contain an examination of one form of contemporary religion. I originally set out to gain some insight into what middle America is doing with its traditional commitment to Christianity. In the course of my investigations, I found that the social location of meaning-giving and moral authority was a pressing issue for many believers. In the community I studied, this issue was raised with critical urgency as a result of secular events which were not merely local and parochial but which originated in national trends of the late 1960s.

Among the religious devices believers used to respond to the crises of that time and that place was the creation of what I call interaction ritual. In interaction ritual, believers shifted the social location of meaning-giving and moral authority from hierarchical and centralized authorities to the shared charisma of an interacting we-group.

A full understanding of interaction ritual demands that we understand the context of its emergence as fully as possible. Therefore, the main point of this study comes into clear focus only near the half-way mark of the discussion. But there is a point about method in the slow build-up of the discussion: There is no quick and easy way to diagnose the central tendencies of any social situation. The reward of grounded insight justifies the discipline of methodical observation.

Sunday Morning

CHAPTER 1

Sunday Morning

The patterns of American religion have undergone profound changes since the early 1960s. The popularity of Asian philosophies, the increasingly open cultivation of occult practices, the losses of membership, revenues, and clergy in the mainline denominations, and the startling changes in Roman Catholicism—all contribute to a picture of change that seems to have the depth and scope of that of the Protestant Reformation.

This study examines one aspect of this picture of change: an aspect which has been generally neglected, yet which seems to be of central importance. If we want to understand the basis for current changes in religion and the direction they are taking, it would seem logical to examine religious ritual; for ritual—how a group worships—is the fullest expression of that group's fundamental religious orientations. Ritual is the behavior, the act, the gesture toward transcendence which reveals more accurately and more completely than any other religious phenomenon the meaning of a religious commitment.

Most current interest in religious changes in the United States focuses on the new forms of religion which are replacing the old forms. This is change by substitution: one whole system is discarded and another is set in its place. Thus, when Bellah discusses the religion of a "post-traditional age," he tends to emphasize the discontinuity between what has gone before and what is currently arising.[1] Studies based on this focal interest view ritual as a taken-for-granted

---

[1] Robert N. Bellah, *Beyond Belief: Religion in a Post-traditional Age* (New York: Harper and Row, 1970).

1

constant. When a new form of religion is adopted or invented, it has "of course" a new form of ritual.

In my investigation of Sunday morning worship services at four churches in Chicago, I found a different phenomenon. This was the radical and structural change of the traditional form of worship in a congregation of a mainline Protestant denomination. This change occurred, moreover, in interaction with local and national social events. We have here a case of transition rather than of simple substitution. In this process of religious change, the central issue was the form and content of ritual. The ritual changed and, with it, the religion. In this case, ritual appears as the expression of the essence of religion, and such other aspects of religion as stated beliefs, social policies, and political activities appear to be epiphenomenal in comparison.

RELIGIOUS BELIEFS AND SOCIAL CHANGE

In a recent scholarly article, Roy and his colleagues state at the outset, "The relationship between socioeconomic status and religious belief continues to be a central topic of inquiry in the sociology of religion."[2] And a review article dealing with the work of Charles Y. Glock points out that one of Glock's main contributions to the sociology of religion was that he "paid attention to the content of religious belief," treating it as an independent variable rather than as a result of other social processes.[3]

Glock's contribution is surely admirable, but we must move on, for the use of stated beliefs as the most valid indicator of the nature of religion in surely incorrect. This has been evident since Freud's *Interpretation of Dreams* became part of Western intellectual currency. Behavior also has meaning, and the interpretation of action and gesture is indispensable for the full understanding of any social phenomenon. This is one reason why ethnographic techniques of participant observation must always complement survey research in the sociological tradition.

The sociology of religion in America has been mainly the province

[2] R. F. Van Roy, F. D. Bean, Jr., and R. Wood, "Social Mobility and Doctrinal Orthodoxy," *Journal for the Scientific Study of Religion* 12 (1973): 427.

[3] Barbara W. Hargrove, Russell R. Dynes, and William M. Newman, "The Sociology of Religion of Charles Y. Glock," *Journal for the Scientific Study of Religion* 12 (1973): 456.

of survey researchers, and the bias of the method has determined that the discussion of religion and social change, for example, be cast in the idiom of *religious beliefs* and ____; the phrase is completed by filling in the blank with any of the social phenomena survey research can handle: race, age, political activism, attitudes toward civil rights, use of drugs, and so on. Ritual, in this kind of study, appears as an answer to the question "How often do you go to church?" The ritual dimension of religion in Glock's research, for example, is a frequency distribution of attendance at ritual.[4] It says nothing about what the churchgoers do when they get to church. But since behavior has meaning over and above the meaning of stated beliefs, what they do at church is of central importance.

The questions of where religion comes from and why it changes can be probed to their foundations only by techniques which include direct observations. The focus on beliefs characteristic of survey research can lead to false conclusions. An example is the following comment on recent changes in American religion:

> The heart of this revolution is the demise of what for nearly two thousand years has been proclaimed as the core of Christian faith: a literal interpretation of the phrase, "Christ crucified, risen, coming again."[5]

Taken at face value, this statement is simply wrong. If what the authors mean to say is that this change in the expression of religious beliefs is a very important *symptom* of some underlying dynamic of change, then it is correct. But to mistake the symptom for the "heart" is an important error. Such an overstatement indicates that survey research techniques need to be supplemented.

THE ANALYSIS OF RITUAL

The analysis of ritual has long been the concern of anthropologists, but they have seldom studied ritual which is changing. For anthropologists generally deal with traditional and stable societies. They have been fascinated by the manner in which ritual reveals important features of the cultural and social patterns of those societies. Since the societies were stable, the rituals appeared as constants. This point

---

[4] See Rodney Stark and Charles Y. Glock, *American Piety: The Nature of Religious Commitment* (Berkeley: University of California Press, 1968).

[5] Ibid., p. 276.

is underscored by Geertz's classic analysis of a *slametan* in Java.[6] Geertz points out:

> There was no argument over whether the slametan pattern was the correct ritual, whether the neighbors were obligated to attend, or whether the supernatural concepts upon which the ritual was based were valid ones. For both the santris and the abangans in the kampongs, the slametan maintains its force as a genuine sacred symbol; it still provides a meaningful framework for facing death—for most people the only meaningful framework.[7]

In the phenomenon Geertz encountered, social patterns had changed, but the ritual did not change. Even though the constancy of the ritual thus becomes an intriguing social and cultural issue, it is still constancy which characterizes the ritual in question.

In the *slametan*, "There was no argument over whether [it] was the correct ritual." In the case presented here, such an argument is of central importance. Geertz, Victor Turner, and many other anthropologists have long known the importance of religious ritual, and they have refined the techniques of analysis. All I am doing, in a sense, is transferring the site of investigation from Africa or Java to a residential neighborhood in a midwestern American city. One effect of this change of site is to raise the issue of ritual change and social change, not just ritual and social change.

DATA AND METHOD

In the following pages we shall examine the Sunday morning worship services of four white, middle-class churches in Lincoln Park, a cosmopolitan urban neighborhood of Chicago, in the late 1960s. In one of these—the Church of the Three Crosses—the service underwent profound change between 1964 and 1970. In another church—St. Paul—some members of the congregation experimented with changes similar to those which occurred in Three Crosses. These experiments took place between 1968 and 1971. The worship service in two other nearby churches—St. James and St. Clement—did not change structurally during the period of study (1969–1970).

These four churches are known to me from my two-year residence

---

[6]Clifford Geertz, "Ritual and Social Change: A Javanese Example," *American Anthropologist* 59 (1957): 32-53.

[7]Ibid., p. 49.

in the area. In that time I became a member of the congregation of the Church of the Three Crosses and was known to other members as an inquisitive participant doing research on religious ritual. I took an active part in the ritual and congregational life of this church and also participated in many discussions and meetings with members of the congregation of St. Paul. I taught for one year at the magnet church school conducted on its premises. My research in the two other churches—St. James and St. Clement—was limited to attendance at Sunday worship on several occasions and tape-recorded conversations with the pastors and some lay members of the congregations.

The data for this study came from many sources, as is usual for ethnographic research, but the (main source was my observation in detail of the ritual performances themselves.) Observations were made in all four churches as well as in the surrounding community. These observations were especially important for providing detailed information on the worship services and the congregations' responses to them. They were also important for describing the social ecology of the community area and the responses of congregations and individual churchgoers to the secular affairs of the nation and the local area.

(A second source of data was interviews conducted with the pastors of all the churches and with many members of the congregations.) They ranged from formal question-and-answer exchanges to casual conversations. The substance of many of these conversations was recorded in the form of summary notes. Some interviews were tape-recorded. In these conversations I asked specific questions intended to capture in condensed form the substance of more informal exchanges. I conducted and transcribed fifteen such interviews, each approximately ninety minutes long. Nine were with pastors or members of the Church of the Three Crosses, five were with pastors or members of St. Paul, and one was with the pastor and a lay member of St. James Church.

(Third, documents were used to construct a history of each church and of the community and to verify some of the information obtained in interviews.)

The student of religious ritual to whom I am principally indebted for developing a technique for analyzing ritual is Victor W. Turner. In the course of his study of Ndembu ritual in East Africa, Turner observes:

> When we talk about the meaning of a symbol, we must be careful to distinguish between at least three levels or fields of meaning. These I propose

to call: (1) the level of indigenous interpretation (or, briefly, the exegetical meaning), (2) the operational meaning, and (3) the positional meaning.[8]

The exegetical meaning is what people say the ritual means. The operational meaning is what can be inferred from what they do in ritual. The positional meaning is what can be inferred from the position of ritual elements in spatial arrangements.[9]

MASS RITUAL AND INTERACTION RITUAL

Observation and analysis of rituals in the four churches I studied led me to make a distinction between what I have chosen to call mass ritual and interaction ritual. Mass ritual is so designated because in its performance there is an audience that responds to the presentation of the sacred symbols as a unified body, a mass. Interaction ritual is so called because in its performance participants do not merely react to the presentation of sacred symbols but interact among themselves without the dominant initiative of religious specialists. They modify the presentation as it unfolds. They also interact with one another in the process of constructing the ritual.[10]

[8] Victor W. Turner, *The Forest of Symbols: Aspects of Ndembu Ritual* (Ithaca, N.Y.: Cornell University Press, 1967), p. 50.

[9] Karl Mannheim also has a three-level conceptual scheme for analyzing ritual. His antedates Turner's by about forty years and is meant to apply to any cultural product, not just ritual. Turner's terminology calls more attention to the psychological status—conscious or unconscious—of the levels of meaning, and Mannheim's terminology calls more attention to the cultural ramifications of the levels of meaning. But both men agree that the interpretation of cultural products such as religious ritual requires attention to hidden meanings. See Karl Mannheim, *Essays on the Sociology of Knowledge,* ed. Paul Kecskeneti (London: Routledge and Kegan Paul, 1952), pp. 37–61.

[10] During the final stages of this study, I engaged in lengthy discussions on the appropriate labels for these two kinds of ritual. The chief defect of the labels used is that they focus on superficial properties of the rituals: what they "feel like" on first acquaintance with them. It would be better, it was argued, to label them by salient analytical properties. A change in these labels would also avoid confusion with similar terms such as *the Mass* for Roman Catholic ritual and *interaction ritual* as used by Erving Goffman.

However, the analytic implications of the differences between the two kinds of ritual extend in many directions. Besides the fact that other terms seemed clumsy and unnecessarily esoteric, the surface labels may serve to leave the implications open rather than force analysis into premature closure. As for the similarity to Goffman's term, we will have to live with that, for the similarity is not without foundation. Goffman's phrase points to the ritualistic aspects of interaction, and what the phrase means here is the interactional nature of a formal ritual.

The two kinds of ritual are different at all three levels of meaning. At the exegetical level, participants in mass ritual say that it presents "objective revelation," that it portrays a sacred cosmos "which man has very little to do with." Participants in interaction ritual say that it is "one, two, or five people saying what that scripture really means to them." They feel that ritual is a process in which each person interacts with and modifies traditional symbols and rites to create new meanings.

At the operational level, mass ritual is compartmental. In particular, the role of initiating sacred action or utterance is assigned to specially marked and segregated persons, mainly the clergy. The compartments of mass ritual clearly distinguish between the sacred cosmos with its manifestations and the profane world with its manifestations. There are clear distinctions between sacred and secular music, between sacred writing (the Bible, in these cases) and secular writing, between sacred roles and secular roles (clergy and laity). The operational meaning of interaction ritual is communitarian and synthetic. The role of initiating sacred utterance or action is assigned by the congregation to various of its members at random. Those who may wish to give a sermon get their turn. Artists make banners, musicians compose and play songs. In this respect there is no distinction between clergy and laity. Sacred music includes whatever songs members of the congregation find meaningful, whether the Beatles or Bach. In addition to the Bible, readings are performed from contemporary books, magazines, and newspapers. In sum, there is no compartmentalization of the symbols of the sacred and the symbols of the profane. In interaction ritual, any artifact, even something as prosaic and mundane as a plastic wrapper for a loaf of bread, can be a symbol of the sacred.

At the positional level, mass ritual is also compartmental. The

---

The central difference between mass ritual and interaction ritual is the social location they assign to meaning-giving and moral authority. Thus they could be called hierarchical ritual and egalitarian ritual, or tradition ritual and charismatic ritual. But such pairs of terms do not immediately add any clarity and would have to be explained as thoroughly as the terms I have chosen. The terms which seemed to be the best candidates for substitution were *ritual of security* and *ritual of discovery*. But these are needlessly ideological. If discovery and security are correctly counterposed purposes of the two kinds of ritual, that will be clear from the analysis.

Since the issues raised by the distinction are so complex, it seemed best to keep the intuitive and superficial labels. At least others interested in the phenomenon will know what I am pointing at, and that is enough to get the analysis started.

space for ritual is a special room or part of a room set aside for the performance of ritual only. Moreover, within this space, there is a more sacred zone and a less sacred zone, with a fencelike partition marking the boundary between them. The clergy move in the more sacred zone, and the laity stay in the less sacred zone. The positional meaning of interaction ritual is fluid. The ritual space has a permeable center of low salience, whose boundaries are unmarked. The room for ritual can also be used for other purposes, and ritual can be performed outdoors in the park in good weather.

THE SOCIAL CONTEXT OF THE TWO KINDS OF RITUAL

The reasons for the occurrence of mass ritual and interaction ritual are intimately connected with the function of ritual: to give meaning to the experience of everyday life. Interaction ritual emerged because Lincoln Park in the late 1960s was in a potentially anomic situation. Through the process of urban renewal, energetically pushed by city authorities, hundreds of buildings were being torn down and their occupants moved out. Marches and demonstrations were taking place, "radicals" were active, and there were even times when tear gas wafted into living rooms. In the summer of 1968 the community was the scene of one of the most important political demonstrations of the era—the activity surrounding the convention of the Democratic party.

In the midst of this conflict and chaos, some religious believers looked to traditional symbols and authorities for the meaning of the events and found those sources wanting. Instead of leaving the church, they tried to create a form of ritual which would enable their traditional Christian commitment to speak more directly to the events going on in the community. The process they devised was essentially a dispersal and a sharing of charismatic authority, in which meaning was to be found through each person's saying what the scripture meant to him or her.

One might ask why some rituals changed and others did not, since all the believers were equally exposed—by virtue of their common environment—to urban renewal and the demonstrations. This is a complex question, and to answer it we must look at the history of each congregation, its cultural background and organizational traditions. We find, for example, that the Church of the Three Crosses sprang from a denomination with populist origins in the eighteenth and nineteenth centuries. The reawakening of the latent cultural option of charismatic dissent from the pronouncements of central authorities was therefore easier for the members of this congregation than for some others. The shared charisma of interaction ritual bears some resemblance to the Quaker meetings of the seventeenth century.[11]

But the emergence of interaction ritual in Lincoln Park must also be seen as a distinctly contemporary phenomenon. Scholars and churchmen have noted a malaise of the mainline denominations all over the country. Urban renewal in this neighborhood was just one more important social phenomenon to which the church found it hard to give meaning. In the late 1960s, churches were divided and enervated by their efforts to judge the moral properties of the civil rights movement, the Vietnam war, and the feared flight of youth to the "counterculture." Because of these issues, many were disposed to doubt the usefulness of traditional and established meaning-giving authorities. One of the breaks from established tradition was the creation of interaction ritual.

If we examine the two forms of ritual closely, we find that the central import of their difference is the change in the social location of meaning-giving and moral authority. The question for the religious believer is "How do I decide whether it is good or evil?" The "it," of course, can be urban renewal, a political demonstration, a civil rights march, draft resistance, the Marxist rhetoric of a black or Puerto Rican organization, the emergence of the hippie, and so on. If the bishop, the church, the pastor, the mayor, and the president all fail to give a satisfactory answer, then one option for the believer is to look to his or her own inner light and that of fellow-believers for the answers. This is what interaction ritual enables the believer to do.

In the chapters which follow, I shall first describe the social and

[11] During its first hundred years of existence (approximately 1660 to 1760), the Society of Friends in England and the Colonies conducted various kinds of prayer meetings. The radically egalitarian form of the Quaker meeting—in which the Inner Light of each participant has equal power to break the silence—was only one form. Various kinds of hierarchy continually crept into Quaker meetings. In Pennsylvania in the eighteenth century, not only was there a hierarchy of persons within some meetings, but a hierarchy of meetings themselves. Among contemporary Friends, there are meetings with clergy and sermon and hymns which are like the worship services of any mainline denomination. There are also interaction rituals of the Inner Light. The Quakers are one of the few—if not the only—religious groups in the modern West to cultivate actively the rite I call interaction ritual.

historical context—the community area called Lincoln Park; then the
general institutional background of the rituals; and then the social
and doctrinal background of the four churches included in the study.
I shall then present a detailed description of the mass ritual and interaction ritual observed in these churches. Finally, I shall discuss the
social sources and larger implications of the occurrence of interaction
ritual in its context.

CHAPTER 2

The Demonstration Capital of the World

The community area of Lincoln Park lies on the north side of Chicago, from two to three and a half miles north of the center of the city, between Lake Michigan and the north branch of the Chicago River. (See figure 1.) Its southern and northern boundaries are North Avenue and Diversey Parkway, respectively. Within this formally defined community area is a slightly smaller area often identified as Lincoln Park by residents because of its selection as a "General Neighborhood Renewal Plan" area by the Chicago Department of Urban Renewal in 1956.

The larger area was defined as a "community area" by University of Chicago sociologists in the 1930s. The designation is therefore somewhat artificial. The area has certain close relationships with the areas just south and north of it and has important internal divisions.

In relation to contiguous areas, Lincoln Park is joined closely to the "Near North Side." The public high school in the community—Waller High School—draws many students from the Cabrini-Green Homes, a Chicago Housing Authority project which in 1967 contained a population of almost 18,000 persons, almost all of them black, in 3,581 dwelling units. Bordering the east side of Lincoln Park, the Near North Side is heavily populated by young white apartment dwellers, highly mobile and relatively affluent. The east side of Lincoln Park is thus a virtual continuation of the residential and cultural patterns of the Near North Side.

The community area of Lake View lies to the north of Lincoln Park. Toward Lake Michigan, on the east side of these areas, the

FIGURE 1. Outline Map of the City of Chicago

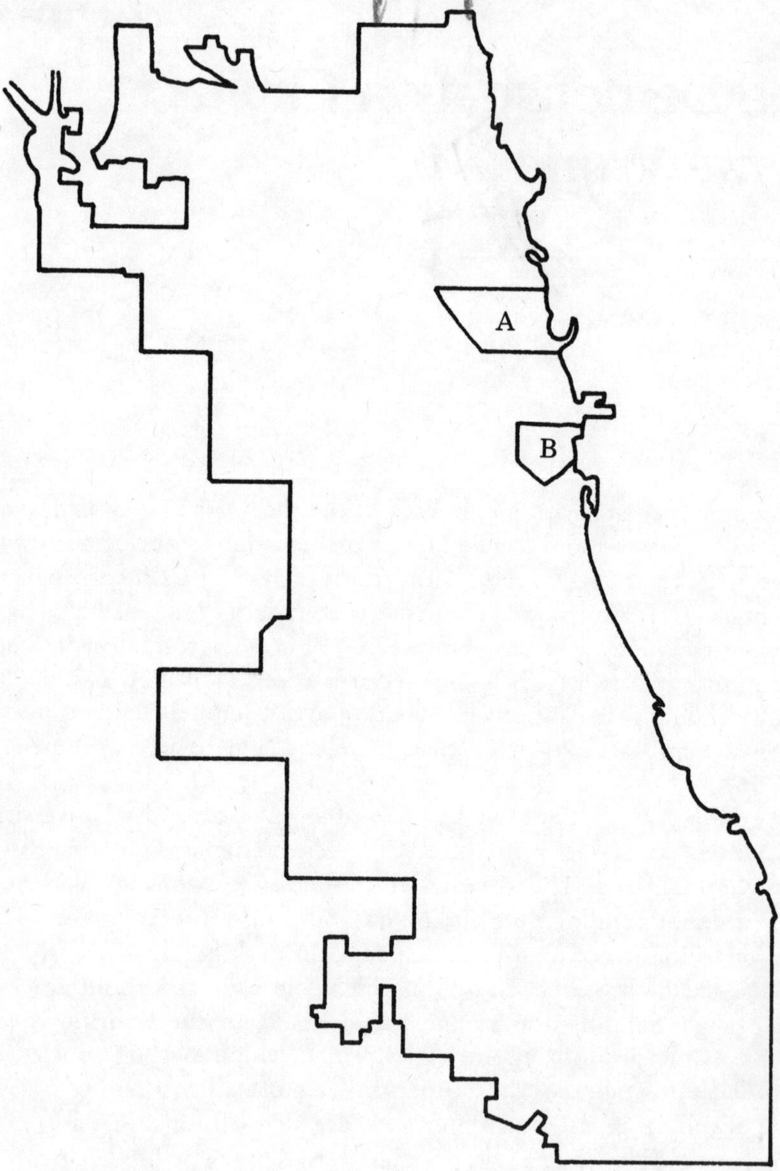

A—Lincoln Park
B—Central Business District ("the Loop")

settlement pattern is again homogeneous: young adult apartment dwellers, the heaviest concentration of Jewish residents of these areas, and the most mobile and affluent of the local whites. Toward the west—roughly west of Halsted Street—the two areas are also homogeneous. This is an area of lower-middle-class ethnic groups, from the oldest settlers (Germans) through the second-wave arrivals (Slavs, Hungarians, etc.) to the most recent arrivals (Japanese, American Indians, Asian Indians).

Lincoln Park is thus a very heterogeneous neighborhood, with blacks and Puerto Ricans in the southwest quadrant, white homeowners and affluent apartment dwellers along its east side, old ethnic groups in its northwest quadrant, and through its center (along Lincoln Avenue) an area of small art galleries, experimental theaters, and counterculture meeting places. The persons who staff and frequent these "bohemian" and counterculture centers reside throughout the central portions of the area. This part of Lincoln Park (including almost half the area) is culturally transitional and therefore has indefinite boundaries. Thus the area was quite susceptible to multidimensional conflict when an effort was made to construct programs for the improvement of "the community."

THE HISTORY OF LINCOLN PARK

In 1840 what is now known as the Lincoln Park community was a flat, heavily wooded area between the recently incorporated City of Chicago and the village of Lake View. Little Fort Road ran through this area, heading northwest to the town of Morton Grove. The woods in the area were partially cleared during the mid-nineteenth century, and the land was used for growing vegetable produce for Chicago residents. The early truck farmers were almost exclusively German immigrants, mostly of Protestant faith.[1]

Chicago grew very rapidly in the mid- and late nineteenth century, extending its city limits by a series of land annexations north, south, and west of the central city. Among these annexations was that of "North Town," occurring in two legislative acts, in 1851 and 1853. North Town extended from the old (since 1837) city limits, North Avenue, to the boundary of the town of Lake View (Fullerton Ave-

[1] Vivian Palmer, "History of the North Side of Chicago" (unpublished typescript, Chicago Historical Society, 1932).

nue), between Lake Michigan and the north branch of the Chicago River.

At the time of its annexation in 1863, this area was still rural in character, with the farmhouses of the truck gardeners established along a single main artery, Little Fort Road (changed to Lincoln Avenue in the late 1860s). With the building of bridges across the north branch of the Chicago River in the 1850s, the area became more densely settled. It retained its predominately German character as it became a residential area of small frame houses gradually encroaching on the open fields of the truck farms.

In 1860 a large tract of the still-open land was purchased by Scotch-Irish Presbyterians as the site for their theological seminary. Today McCormick Theological Seminary stands on that site in the center of Lincoln Park. With the founding of the seminary, a community of Scotch-Irish Presbyterians was established in Lincoln Park, composed of the seminary faculty, students, their families, and some truck farmers who were attracted to the area by the presence of their ethnic confreres.

Even at this stage of the area's growth, before it was fully developed, there were civic and real-estate interests who wanted the lakefront area developed into recreational space. A few of these local leaders obtained a city ordinance in 1864 declaring the natural sand dunes and beaches between North Avenue and the city limits (Fullerton) to be a public park. The cemetery at the south end of this area was gradually removed (the last graves were moved in 1874). The park was originally called Lake Park, but the name was changed to Lincoln Park in the following year, 1865, in memory of the recently assassinated president. Little Fort Road became Lincoln Avenue soon after. Eventually the residential area assumed the name of the park and the street.

In 1871 the Great Fire destroyed almost all the frame structures in the area, and the following year the City of Chicago passed a zoning ordinance requiring that all buildings replacing those destroyed by fire be built of brick or stone. This ordinance was often violated, but it nonetheless helped create a basis for the development of different socioeconomic areas in the neighborhood. More substantial and expensive buildings were erected on the east side of the area, while working-class people were still able to build cheaper frame houses on the west side. (See figure 2.)

After the Great Fire, building proceeded at a rapid pace, so that the area was residentially mature by 1895. Over 90 percent of the

FIGURE 2. Land-use Zones of Lincoln Park

1–Factory Area   3–Area of Brick Structures
2–Area of Mostly Frame Houses 4–The Park

structures existing in Lincoln Park in 1960 were built between 1872 and 1895.

During the 1870s and 1880s the first development of industry occurred in the area. Before the Great Fire, Lincoln Park had known only farming and residential development, but after the fire, furniture and other wood-products manufacturing enterprises were developed on the east bank of the Chicago River. (Local timber was still available.) In the 1880s other industries followed. Following the building of these factories, new waves of multiethnic immigration took place. Poles, Slavs, Rumanians, and Hungarians moved into the area, mainly west of the German settlement east of Racine Street.

A small Irish settlement grew up along Fullerton just west of the Presbyterian seminary. St. Vincent Catholic Church was founded in this small enclave in 1875. As the Irish thrived, the settlement became the site of St. Vincent's College, now known as DePaul University.

From 1853 to 1889, Fullerton was still the northern boundary of the City of Chicago. When the town of Lake View was annexed in 1889, the heavily settled area between Fullerton and Diversey came to be thought of as part of Lincoln Park.

From the turn of the century the ethnic composition of the area continued to diversify. Improved means of transportation—paved streets and the electrically powered streetcar—made Lincoln Park a desirable residence for people who worked in the central business district and adjacent areas.

World War I had a decided effect on the distinctive German ethos that had prevailed in the neighborhood. The outward manifestations of German culture were curtailed by the anti-German emotions aroused by the war. The weekend activities of the *Turnverein* in the park diminished, and some well-to-do Germans who were attracted to the area by its cultural facilities now had less reason to stay. Nonetheless, as late as 1920, the distinctively German cultural character of the area was still vigorous.

By 1970, however, the external manifestations of this cultural orientation could be found only in the German inscriptions on the stained-glass windows of St. Michael Church, the "Lincoln Turners" gymnasium on Diversey Parkway, the *Gottesdienst* worship service in St. Paul United Church of Christ, John Weiss's Pub with its exclusively German songs on the jukebox, and one small German bakery on Armitage Avenue. But when we examine the churches of the neighborhood, we find signs of a more durable allegiance to the old way.

In 1930 one quarter of the population of the area was still of German ethnic origin. Between the two world wars there was very little residential construction. High-rise buildings were built along Lake View Street, overlooking Lincoln Park. Most of these replaced older three-flat apartment buildings. But some lots continued to be subdivided, and the population continued to increase gradually until the early 1950s. (See table 1.)

TABLE 1. Popu-
lation of Lincoln
Park, 1920–1970

1920	94,247
1930	97,873
1940	100,826
1950	102,996
1960	88,836
1970	67,793

The sharp decline in the area's population after World War II re-
flects the breakup of a stable mosaic of many ethnic communities
and the filling of this ecological vacuum by economically, socially,
and culturally marginal groups: new Spanish-speaking arrivals, artists
and bohemians, and young political dissenters and supporters of the
counterculture. These groups moved into an area of deteriorating
houses and declining commercial and industrial activity. The new
mosaic fed, not on the early-twentieth-century optimism about the
American way, but on the new ambivalence about American political
power and the cultural investment in technology characteristic of the
1960s.

AFTER WORLD WAR II

After World War II the problem of urban blight, which affects all
major American cities, began to be felt in Lincoln Park. Many frame
buildings dating back to the 1890s were in a state of severe deterioration. Newer and poorer ethnic groups took up residence in the area.
The presence of Spanish-speaking people from Mexico, Puerto Rico,
and the American Southwest was becoming quite visible. Although
the minuscule settlement of black people in the southwest corner of
Lincoln Park had not grown to the extent that other black concen-
trations in the city had, the area just south of Lincoln Park, around
Division and Larrabee streets, was already predominately black and
very overcrowded.[2]

[2] This area was transformed into housing projects by the Chicago Housing
Authority in three stages. The Cabrini Homes (585 dwelling units) were completed in 1942. The Cabrini Homes extension (1,900 dwelling units) was completed in 1958 during the great boom in housing in housing-project construction.

The first sign of community concern for these new problems was the rise of neighborhood and community organizations. The Old Town Triangle Association was started in 1948, the Mid-North Association in 1950. (See figure 3.) In the same year representatives of social-service organizations in Lincoln Park formed the Lincoln Park Welfare Community Council. These groups began to organize to clean up their neighborhoods, get building codes enforced, and improve the effectiveness of social-service facilities.

The activities of these groups were observed closely and to some extent supported by the major semi-public institutions in Lincoln Park. These included some of the churches, the four large hospitals (Children's Memorial, Grant, Augustana Lutheran, and Columbus), Aetna Bank, McCormick Seminary, and DePaul University. (See figure 4.)

Also under close observation were the events taking place on the south side of Chicago in Hyde Park–Kenwood. Peter Rossi and Robert Dentler have produced a detailed account of the "roads to conservation and renewal" in Hyde Park–Kenwood during the years of decision, the mid-1950s. The Hyde Park–Kenwood Urban Renewal Plan was approved by the Chicago City Council in 1958. Its implementation was completed by the early 1960s, thanks to the power, energy, and skill of the University of Chicago, which used its resources to overcome the "primitive state of governmental machinery in the city before 1956"[3] and push for a quick restoration of its environs to middle-class status.

In Lincoln Park, the process moved much more slowly. Twenty-two years after the founding of the first neighborhood organization in 1948, contracts for Phase I of the renewal plan for Lincoln Park were still under consideration. And when the Department of Urban Renewal made approvals on February 11, 1970, a small riot broke out in the chamber of the City Council, and several residents of Lincoln Park were arrested. Clearly, tensions similar to those described by Rossi and Dentler were present in Lincoln Park. These tensions were most acute in the years 1966–1970 and became—in the minds

---

The Green Homes (1,096 dwelling units) were completed in 1962. The total population of these projects in 1967 was approximately 18,000 persons, occupying 70 acres of land—one fourth the area of all Lincoln Park. Waller High School and Arnold Upper Grade Center, both in Lincoln Park, served the children of Cabrini-Green and thus stimulated a close relationship between the projects and the Lincoln Park community area.

[3] Peter H. Rossi and Robert A. Dentler, *The Politics of Urban Renewal* (Glencoe, Ill.: Free Press, 1961), p. 276.

FIGURE 3. Neighborhood Organizations in Lincoln Park

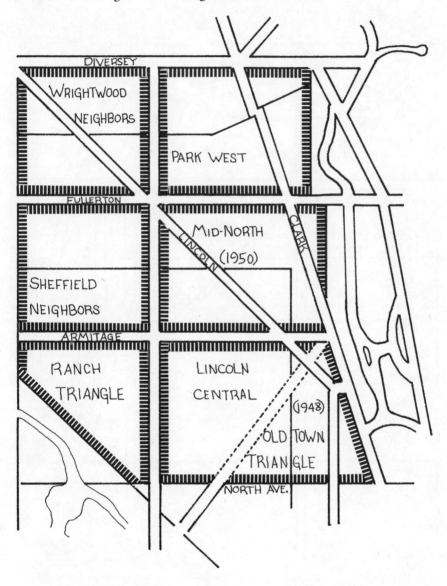

of many residents of the area—intimately connected with national and international political and cultural cleavages. The churches of Lincoln Park gave a variety of political, economic, and ritual responses to these tensions. We shall be concerned primarily with their specifically religious, ritual responses.

FIGURE 4. Major Semi-public Institutions

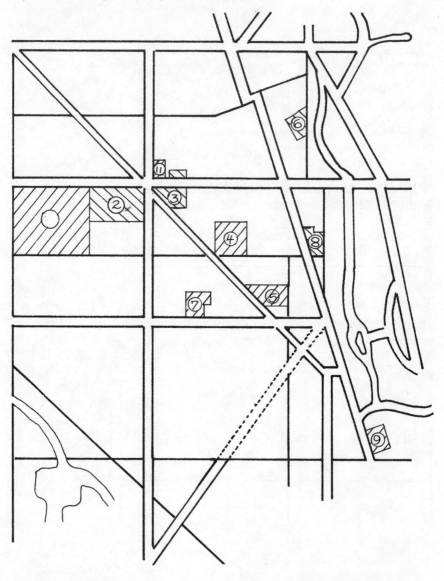

1—DePaul University
2—McCormick Theological
   Seminary
3—Children's Memorial Hospital
4—Grant Hospital
5—Augustana Lutheran Hospital
6—Columbus Hospital

7—Waller High School and
   Arnold Upper Grade Center
8—Francis Parker High School
9—Chicago Historical Society
10—Lincoln Park
11—Aetna Bank

By the time urban renewal reached Lincoln Park, local conflicts were no longer seen as merely local. Those who felt themselves excluded from the benefits of urban renewal defined the issues in ideological terms rather than in terms of local benefits and losses. Parties to the local conflict were called "capitalist oppressors" and "Marxist revolutionaries." This superimposition of international and ideological conflicts on local and real-estate conflicts was at least rhetorical and symbolic, and to some degree—hard to measure—also real. Some opponents of urban renewal did in fact identify themselves with the National Liberation Front of Vietnam. Some supporters of moderate-income housing did in fact see the North Side Cooperative Ministry as Communist in orientation.

In the late 1960s, Lincoln Park was richer in political and cultural diversity than most urban communities. Besides the racial mix of black, Spanish-speaking, old ethnic whites, and middle-class cosmopolitan whites, there was the cultural mix of artist-bohemian-hippie (and "radical") with business-oriented white-collar workers. Lincoln Avenue became in the early 1960s one of the principal centers of the counterculture in Chicago. Along with the small art galleries and "head shops" came the underground newspapers and the political organizers. The offices of *The Seed* (Chicago's most durable underground newspaper) and of *Rising Up Angry* (an underground newspaper and organizing group working with young lower-middle-class whites, were located on Lincoln Avenue, as was the meeting hall of the Industrial Workers of the World ("Wobblie Hall"), the office of the Concerned Citizens of Lincoln Park, and the counterculture's principal entertainment spot, Alice's Restaurant (renamed Alice's Revisited in 1971).

In the summer of 1968, the residents of Lincoln Park smelled tear gas, wafted into the community by an easterly breeze from the green lawns of Lincoln Park proper. On the night of August 27, hundreds of young people—"hippies, yippies, and radicals"—battled Chicago police, and in the midst of the fray were twenty-odd clergymen from the community of Lincoln Park and from Lake View to the north. Some of the demonstrators at the Democratic Convention slept in local churches which had been turned into temporary dormitories for the occasion. The congregations of these churches discovered unsuspected cleavages among their own members as a result of this action.

When in the fall of the next year the Weatherman faction of Students for a Democratic Society staged its "days of rage," Lincoln

Park was the staging ground. At a meeting of community residents, clergymen, and Chicago police called to help mitigate the impact of the Weathermen's demonstration, one resident referred to the area as the "demonstration capital of the world."

The main event of the convention demonstrations occurred on August 28 in Grant Park, in front of the Conrad Hilton Hotel. But the action of the previous night in Lincoln Park was an integral part of this violent expression of cultural and political differences in American life. For the residents of the Lincoln Park community, these events did not so much draw national attention to the local community area as they drew the attention of the local community residents to the relationship of their own conflicts to national and international conflicts and cleavages.

Pressure to take sides in the conflict was imposed immediately and urgently on the residents of the community. For them the questions were. How shall we use our church premises? How shall we protect our homes? In what role should we participate, or should we stay out of it altogether? The conflicts initiated by leadership cadres of political and cultural activists invaded the everyday life of the citizens and churchgoers of Lincoln Park. Thus they had to make decisions and probe the issues relevant to such decisions.

THE INTERNAL SEGMENTATION OF
LINCOLN PARK

These conflicts are the social setting for the rituals and associations attended by churchgoers in Lincoln Park. In order to describe this social field with some clarity, I shall try to specify the actors or groups in conflict.

A recent observer of political life in the neighborhood[4] has selected "five categoric groups" as the main actors in the community: (1) white middle-class and lower-middle-class homeowners, (2) ethnic minorities, (3) small businessmen, (4) officials of companies with factories in the area, and (5) the semi-public institutions. The list should include (6) adherents to the counterculture, such as the staffs of underground newspapers, members of radical political groups, and the residents of communes.

With this list as a guide, we can specify six distinctive geographic

[4] Rod Paolini, "The Lincoln Park Conservation Association" (M.A. thesis, Northwestern University, June 1970).

areas in Lincoln Park which are expressive of the many-sided social cleavages existing in the community. Five of them are inhabited, and one is the uninhabited area, the cleared land, created by the process of urban renewal in the late 1960s. They are (1) the area of immediate influence of major semi-public institutions, (2) the area of ethnic minorities, (3) the area of white homeowners, (4) the area of the counterculture, (5) the disputed territory, and (6) the factory area. (See figure 5.)

THE MAJOR INSTITUTIONS

On March 29, 1954, the Lincoln Park Conservation Association was formed at a meeting attended by representatives of the Aetna Bank, McCormick Theological Seminary, DePaul University, the Welfare Community Council, the Old Town Triangle Association, and the Mid-North Association, five hospitals (Alexian Brothers, Children's Memorial, Grant, Augustana Lutheran, and Columbus), and some "community leaders."[5] The institutions in this group are the major ones of Lincoln Park.[6] Their resources are neither so great nor so unified as those of the University of Chicago. Therefore, their control of the process of urban renewal has been less sure than the University's was in Hyde Park–Kenwood. They are, however, interested in similar goals, especially the maintenance of their immediate environment as a middle-class neighborhood, with a stable population, low crime rates, and housing suitable for their staff and clients.

These institutions are also corporations and therefore participate in the mainstream of the social orientations of business establishments. Even though all of them except the Aetna Bank are service corporations not run for profit, their style of decisionmaking is hierarchical, impersonal, and highly respondent to other corporate struc-

[5] Ibid., p. 11.

[6] As mentioned above, DePaul University was founded in 1898 as St. Vincent's College. In the 1960s it was a college serving the upwardly mobile working-class Catholic young people of the Chicago area, and drew only a very small percentage of its students from the Lincoln Park community area. The university also has a downtown center, which houses its business school and its law school. Chicago folklore has it that 75 percent of the judges and two-thirds of the aldermen in the city are graduates of DePaul Law School. Mayor Daley is also an alumnus. In 1970 the DePaul University Alumni Association named States Attorney William Hanrahan—also a DePaul alumnus—as their Man of the Year, after his celebrated raid on the Black Panthers apartment in which two Panthers, Fred Hampton and Mark Clark, were killed.

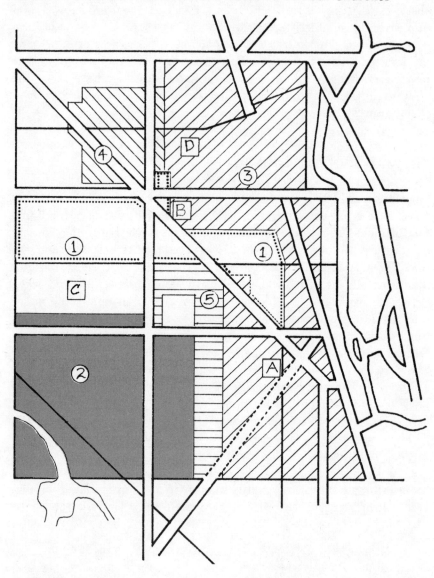

FIGURE 5. Subcultural Areas and Location of Four Churches

1—Major Institutions   A—Church of the Three Crosses
2—Ethnic Minorities   B—St. Paul
3—White Homeowners   C—St. James
4—Counterculture   D—St. Clement
5—Disputed Territory
6—Factories

tures in society. Thus there was underlying tension in Lincoln Park between the interests of institutions which were corporate in structure and those of groups of persons who were merely cultural or socioeconomic entities, not well organized, without substantial political and economic resources, and yet with distinctive interests and value orientations.

Some of these institutions had been the objects of demonstrations. DePaul University was presented with a demand for a day-care center by the Young Lords Organization. McCormick Seminary was occupied twice by the Poor People's Coalition. Demonstrators demanded that Grant Hospital cease providing "back door" health services for the poor and ethnic minorities of the community. But direct confrontations were rare between the institutions of the area and those who feel treated unfairly by them.

In the conflict over urban renewal, the major institutions remained —except on the few occasions mentioned—one symbolic step removed from the arena. The focal point of the struggle was, rather, the community organization which the institutions had initiated—the Lincoln Park Conservation Association.

The LPCA became the "grass roots" organization that passed on the wishes of the community to the organization which officially represented it: the Lincoln Park Community Conservation Council.[7] The CCC, as it came to be called, then passed the community's wishes on to the relevant governmental agency. But for residents of Lincoln Park it was the LPCA that came to stand for all that is best and worst in American political and economic structures. On the one hand, it stood for the right of local groups and individual citizens to organize and affect the decision making of larger political structures. On the other hand, it revealed the hidden basis of this right to organize: the possession of property, of economic surplus to fund the administration of such a lobby, and of access to political structures through traditional or economic ties with established political structures.

In 1956 Lincoln Park was declared a planning area for a General Neighborhood Renewal Plan. In 1961 the plan for the area was reviewed by the federal government's Department of Housing and Home Finance (since renamed the Department of Housing and Urban Development). In March and June of 1962, respectively, the general plan was approved by the Lincoln Park Community Conservation

[7]The Community Conservation Council has fourteen members, seven appointed by the mayor of Chicago and seven elected locally.

Council and the City of Chicago. Funds for detailed planning were approved in 1963 and authorized in 1965, and execution of Phase I for Lincoln Park was begun in 1966.

During this time the Lincoln Park Conservation Association maintained its membership level at approximately one thousand persons (about 1.3 percent of the population of the area). Paolini observes that this organization—not unlike other community organizations—has a very small "active" membership (about seventy-five persons) and is controlled by an even smaller number (about fourteen persons), who are nonetheless supported by the majority of the membership.[8]

As the problems of urban renewal progressed, the focal issue of cleavage in the community became the amount of low-income housing to be included in the redevelopment. This issue was heatedly discussed in the councils of the LPCA in the mid-1960s. The conflict became public in October 1966, when an article in the *Chicago Tribune* reported criticism of LPCA's development priorities by the Reverend James Reed, president of the Lincoln Park Human Relations Committee[9] and pastor of the Parish of the Holy Covenant. Reed criticized LPCA's list of priorities—which began with the needs for the expansion of DePaul University—for not including any mention of low-income housing. Two months later, the *Lincoln Park Booster* reported the formation of a dissenting community organization, the Concerned Citizens Survival Front. Its first president was a young lawyer, and its office was located at 2512 N. Lincoln Avenue, the office of the pastor of the Parish of the Holy Covenant.

The occasion of this open split was the defeat (by a vote of 16 to 14), on December 8, 1966, of a minority resolution in the Board of Directors of LPCA that a specific quota of low-income housing be placed on the priorities recommended to the Department of Urban Renewal for Lincoln Park. From this time until the rejection of the Poor People's Coalition's bid against the Hartford Construction Company in February 1970, the Concerned Citizens Survival Front was the rallying point for those in Lincoln Park who felt themselves excluded or discriminated against by urban renewal. Patricia Devine and Richard Vission, who more than any others became identified with the public image of Concerned Citizens, staffed the office on Lincoln Avenue, called meetings, published leaflets, and contributed

[8] Paolini, pp. 38–39.

[9] A committee of LPCA. Reed was subsequently (January 1967) forced out of his position as president of the committee.

to the merger of local issues of housing with a political ideology characterized as "radical" by supporters as well as opponents of Concerned Citizens. During those three and a half years, the community cleavage over urban renewal in Lincoln Park took on the characteristics of a two-sided zero-sum conflict: each could win only if the other lost.

The two coalitions were of very unequal power. One included the Lincoln Park Conservation Association, the major institutions of the area, and the white homeowners. The other included the Concerned Citizens Survival Front, the Young Lords Organization, the Latin American Defense Organization, Mothers and Others (MAO), occasionally the Latin Kings, CADRE, Women for Peace, Neighborhood Commons, and many other issue-specific interest groups.

The conflict between these groups was not only over the issue of low-income housing; it was also over how to define the conflict over housing. The Lincoln Park Conservation Association's symbolic characterization of the cleavage was of "the community" versus a small number of violent radicals.[10] The Concerned Citizens' definition of the conflict was of "the people" versus a power elite composed of LPCA, the Department of Urban Renewal, and real-estate speculators.[11]

This ideological cleavage arose from within the community itself. As we shall see, the churches responded to it in different ways. Typically, they either ignored it or took it into religious symbol systems as an important ambiguity calling for direct and religious interpretation.

THE AREA OF ETHNIC MINORITIES

The area of ethnic minorities in Lincoln Park is the southwest section of the community. Most of this section is included in the so-called Ranch Triangle (see figure 4, p. 20). Within Ranch Triangle there is a further distinction between the predominantly black areas on the southern side and immediately east of it and the predominantly Puerto Rican and poor-white northern side of the triangle. Census

[10] *LPCA News,* October 1970, p. 4.

[11] *Lincoln Park Press (Prensa),* January 1970, p. 2. The article is entitled "What Is the Concerned Citizens Survival Front?" This paper was published in bilingual form by the staff of the Concerned Citizens.

TABLE 2. Census Figures by Race, 1930–1970*

Year	BLACK		OTHER	
	Number	Per-centage	Number	Per-centage
1930	143	0.1	—	—
1940	132	0.1	130	0.1
1950	205	0.2	1,648	1.6
1960	1,358	1.5	2,874	3.2
1970	4,904	7.2	3,141	4.6

*Source: Statistics were from Evelyn M. Kitagawa and Karl E. Taeuber, eds., *Local Community Fact Book, Chicago Metropolitan Area, 1960* (Chicago: Chicago Community Inventory, University of Chicago, 1963), p. 29.

figures on the growth of nonwhite minorities in Lincoln Park are shown in table 2.

Urban renewal's land clearance primarily affected the census tracts populated by Puerto Ricans. Although there are still a few Puerto Ricans living south and east of the cleared zone, originally the effect of this pattern of land clearance was to distinguish more clearly the southwest quadrant of Lincoln Park from the other segments of the area. Puerto Ricans also live north of Armitage, but as one approaches DePaul University and McCormick Theological Seminary, the socioeconomic and ethnic character of the population changes.

In central Lincoln Park, the various socioeconomic and ethnic groups are "interdigitated" within blocks. Single buildings are very often homogeneous, but even this degree of homogeneity is not universal. A single block in central Lincoln Park typically contains old Germans, old Irish, Puerto Ricans, blacks, "longhairs," and "straight" young adults. But the first four of these groups are moving out, the "longhairs" are classified as a puzzling but temporary nuisance, and the affluent young adults are moving in. Moreover, the closer one gets to the major institutions, the more the "interdigitation" favors the stable "middle-class" residents.

In the late sixties private real-estate speculators were well aware that the neighborhood north of Armitage was "coming up." Buildings could be bought cheaply, renovated, and rented at twice the prices previous occupants had paid. In mid-1970, however, the sale price of buildings between Armitage and the two institutions just mentioned went up approximately 50 percent. Renovation by private developers and by DePaul University (especially on Bissell Street between Webster and Dickens) has been undertaken since early in 1969.

THE YOUNG LORDS ORGANIZATION

Sometime in March 1969, a young Puerto Rican named José "Cha Cha" Jimenez walked into Armitage Avenue Methodist Church to ask that the church rent office space to the Young Lords Organization. This act may mark the emergence of ideology among ethnic minorities of Lincoln Park.

The Young Lords describe their origins as follows:

> At the beginning, the Young Lords were a street gang, one of the bunch of street gangs that hang around Chicago. They began as a Defense Unit in "el barrio" in 1959. Later everybody split when some leaders were jailed for the same reasons that hundreds of *boricuas* [Puerto Ricans] are being jailed for today: fights, drugs, girls, etc.[12]

In September 1970 a Lords' leaflet commented, "In less than a year, YLO has moved from a social club to a revolutionary organization set on serving and protecting the people."[13]

The former street gang now spoke in Marxist, socialist, revolutionary rhetoric.

> It was not until 1969 that this gang under the leadership of José (Cha Cha) Jimenez understood that they had been deceived, that they had been used by this system . . . for their criminal purposes: extermination of all *boricuas* and the continuity of their conditions as instruments for the development of the capital of a few *yanqui* exploiters. . . . It was then that we understood that our enemy was not the poor white, the poor black or brown that we fought in the streets, but the political powers that maintained these races under the actual conditions of misery and poverty.
>
> The Young Lords passed to being a political organization with the goal of exposing the problems of Puerto Rico (its colonial condition) and the goal of working towards getting the full power in the hands of the poor and oppressed people.[14]

In the spring and summer of 1969 the Young Lords became one of the primary symbols of conflict within Lincoln Park. Out of the

[12] YLO leaflet (ca. October 1969).
[13] YLO leaflet, September 1970, p. 6.
[14] YLO leaflet (n.d.).

barrio of Puerto Rican residence, in existence for thirty years, this group of young people arose, defining the local conflicts of Lincoln Park in terms of national and international political, economic, and cultural issues.

The Young Lords' request for office space from Armitage Avenue Methodist Church was turned down because at the time the church was already renting space to a city youth agency, the Joint Youth Development Committee. At the end of May, the JYDC vacated the church, since its lease was up and the church had expressed its intention of selling the building and investing the proceeds to finance low-income housing.

In May 1969 the Young Lords joined with the Concerned Citizens Survival Front to lead an occupation of the administration building of McCormick Theological Seminary. Their purpose was to demonstrate the need and get the seminary's support for the building of more low-income housing in the urban renewal area of Lincoln Park. Other demands were also made to McCormick, but the main thrust of the occupation was McCormick's support of low-income housing.[15]

On June 8, 1969, the Young Lords again asked the church for office space. This request, along with the proposal to sell the building, was voted down by the congregation on June 8. The Young Lords' response was "You will hear from us." The following Wednesday night, June 11, the Lords "liberated" the church building. The congregation's response to this move was not to call the police, but to enter into new negotiations with the Young Lords. A church report comments: "Because of these negotiations, a number of people left the church and we are now down to a worshipping congregation of about fifteen."[16]

As a result of the negotiations, the Young Lords began to renovate the basement of the church to make it usable as a day-care center. On July 25 the church agreed to rent office space to the organization. The Young Lords decorated the outside walls of the church with large, brightly colored murals depicting the heroes and the purposes of their militant struggle. The City of Chicago responded

[15] The demands on McCormick Seminary were to invest $30,000 in building low-income housing in Lincoln Park, and to donate $5,000 to the Latin American Defense Organization, to the Concerned Citizens Survival Front, to the Young Lords Organization, and for hiring a people's architect to design low-income housing units.

[16] "Report to North Side Cooperative Ministry, an undated mimeographed leaflet from the Armitage Avenue People's (Methodist) Church.

with suits about zoning and building code violations. On August 23, 1969, there was a physical confrontation between the Young Lords Organization and the Chicago police on the occasion of the refusal of the city to grant a permit to block off Armitage Avenue between Halsted and Fremont streets for a Lords-sponsored Puerto Rican street fair.

On August 4, 1969, the cleared land on the northeast corner of Halsted and Armitage was occupied by local residents, led by the Young Lords and a Puerto Rican street gang, the Young Comancheros. Since the spring of that year, people in the community had been hearing about urban renewal's designation of the area as the site for a tennis club. Rumors had it that bids were already being let out to contractors to transform the Halsted-Armitage site into a private club with membership fees of $1,200 annually. The Lords, the Comancheros, and their sympathizers entered the empty lot with picks and shovels, and some homemade playground equipment and signs. They leveled the ground, set up the equipment, and put up a sign which read "People's Park."[17]

Events took a tragic turn when the pastor of the Armitage Avenue People's (Methodist) Church, Bruce Johnson, and his wife, Eugenia, were stabbed to death in their apartment on North Seminary on the night of September 29. The following Wednesday night, a memorial service was held for the Johnsons. The Armitage church and the intersection of Dayton and Armitage streets were filled with about 2,000 local residents. Some had marched to the ceremony through the streets of Lincoln Park with church banners. The bishop of the Northeast Illinois Methodist Conference spoke, as did the Reverend James Reed of the Parish of the Holy Covenant, Pat Devine of the Concerned Citizens Survival Front, and Cha Cha Jimenez of the Lords. Musicians from the Old Town School of Folk Music also participated. The ritual for the memorial ceremony included the prayer spoken by all gathered:

> The bread is rising
> Bread means revolution
> God means revolution
> Murder is no revolution

[17] The city withdrew its plans for immediate development of the site. The developer of the tennis club found another site for the project, on Fullerton Avenue just west of Elston. This site is just west of the Chicago River at this point, and therefore outside the official boundaries of Lincoln Park. The People's Park was still in existence in the summer of 1971.

> Revolution is love
> The radical Jesus is winning
> The world is coming to a new beginning
> Organize for a new world
> The liberated zone is at hand
> Right on!

On Saturday, September 11, the Young Lords, the Young Coman-cheros, and the Latin Kings led a march from the People's Park to Humboldt Park, two and a half miles southwest. This march coincided with the Weatherman demonstration in downtown Chicago during which numerous windows were broken in the central business district, and an assistant corporation counsel, Richard Elrod,[18] suffered a broken neck. The march from People's Park to Humboldt Park involved more than three thousand persons, many of them out-of-town members of the Revolutionary Youth Movement (RYM II) faction of Students for a Democratic Society. Even though the marchers had no permit, they were escorted peacefully for the length of their march by Chicago police.

In December the Lords and the other members of the Poor People's Coalition (PPC) again visited McCormick Theological Seminary and persuaded the students to spend a week in political education seminars rather than go to regular seminary classes, so as to remind Mc-Cormick of the commitments it had made to PPC in the spring and which it had not acted upon.

The time was fast approaching when the Community Conservation Council would have to vote on how much low-income housing would in fact be built on Larrabee Street between Dickens and North Avenue. This vote would take the form of a choice between the bid made by the Poor People's Coalition—which had hired an architect and developed plans for several sites in the project—and the bid of the Hartford Construction Company, which planned to build moderate-income units. The support of McCormick was important both for the raising of funds to pay the architect and to subcontract the bid, if obtained, and for getting the votes of a majority of the fourteen-member Community Conservation Council.

The vote on the Poor People's Coalition bid was taken on January 14, 1970, in the gymnasium of St. Michael's High School, and the PPC bid was preferred over the Hartford Construction Company's, 11 to 2. There was much rejoicing among the Coalition groups, and it looked as if the cause might still have a chance. But on February

---

[18] Elrod was elected sheriff of Cook County in 1972.

11, the Department of Urban Renewal reversed the recommendation of the CCC by a vote of 5 to 0 and awarded the contract in question to the Hartford Construction Company.

In May the Young Lords led a march in commemoration of Manuel Ramos, a Puerto Rican youth killed by an off-duty Chicago policeman on May 4, 1969; but otherwise the summer of 1970 was a quiet one. In the fall, José Jimenez—after being bailed out of jail following his arrest on a misdemeanor—disappeared. The Lords continued to run a breakfast program and a free health clinic in the Armitage Avenue church, but the days of marches, rallies, and occupations seemed to be temporarily over.

The total impact of the Lords on Lincoln Park is hard to assess. At a minimum, however, they were another force indigenous to this community which helped raise local tensions to an ideological level. The Lords and the Concerned Citizens directed the consciousness of their audiences to judgments about the American political system. Puerto Rico's "colonial situation," the Vietnam war, and capitalism became issues connected with discrimination against the poor expressed by the City of Chicago's policies on low-income housing. The image of America was presented as the issue underlying judgments about the image of Lincoln Park.

This conflict was aired in the highest circles of American political life. Lincoln Park, and one of its church organizations, were mentioned in testimony before the Senate Subcommittee on Internal Security in the summer of 1970. The church organization in question was the North Side Cooperative Ministry.

THE AREA OF THE COUNTERCULTURE

The area of the counterculture had no sharp geographical boundaries but was indicated by a number of converging clues, including the impressions of informants, the distribution of communes, the distribution of meeting places, and some physical boundary-defining structures.

This subcultural area had a "main street," part of which was its "commercial, public" sector and part its residential sector. The commercial, public sector was Lincoln Avenue from just south of Belden, extending two and a half blocks northwest to Sheffield-Wrightwood. Its residential sector was Wrightwood Avenue from Sheffield-Lincoln extending east to Halsted. The main street was marked by a cluster of meeting places just south of Belden on Lincoln Avenue, Alice's Revisited on Wrightwood just east of Sheffield-Lincoln, and the Other Cheek Commune on Wrightwood just west of Halsted.

The area of Lincoln Park just north of Fullerton and west of Halsted is "protected" from McCormick Seminary and DePaul University by a series of light industry manufacturers along the north side of Fullerton. It is composed predominantly of frame houses without central heating, thus providing cheap residences for artists, bohemians, and counterculture exponents. It is also the place of refuge for artists and bohemians pushed out of Wells Street ("Old Town") by the commercialization of that area for the tourist trade.

There is little precise information on the distribution of communes; therefore, the designation of the counterculture area of Lincoln Park as the locale of a concentration of such households depends on fragmentary information. In terms of the symbolic life of the community of Lincoln Park, however, this lack of precise information on distribution is not important. What was most apparent to the members of this counterculture was that the Lincoln-Wrightwood section had the reputation for being "cool" and for containing communal households.

THE AREA OF WHITE HOMEOWNERS

Clark Street is the main commercial section of the east side of Lincoln Park. This street features many small fashionable clothing stores called boutiques, along with supermarkets and restaurants. The wards and precincts of the east side are the stronghold of the Independent Precinct Organization, an antimachine group formed by backers of Senator Eugene McCarthy after the 1968 primary elections campaign.

In the late sixties the residential area on both sides of Clark Street had a significantly higher median income and a lower social-disorganization score than the western two-thirds of Lincoln Park. There are very few frame buildings among the high rises, condominiums, and well-kept apartment buildings and homes of this area. Instead of the revolutionary graffiti along Lincoln and Halsted ("Revolutionary Grease," "All Power to the Sisters," "Free Angela Davis," "Fred Lives, Pigs Die"), election time brings out posters of electoral political activity ("Re-elect Singer").

This "cultural zone" of Lincoln Park is, toward its southern end, separated from the area of ethnic minorities by a "disputed area": the cleared land on both sides of Larrabee from North Avenue to the intersection of Webster and Lincoln. Toward its northern end, its boundary is indicated by the change in the general quality of housing structures between Orchard and Burling streets.

THE DISPUTED AREA

In 1970 there was a three-quarter-mile stretch of residential and commercial property along Larrabee Street containing only ten structures. (See figure 5, p. 24.) On the west side of the street stood the Tap Root Pub, a nearly completed fire station, and the office of the Lincoln Park Conservation Area Service Center. On the east side of the street, three houses and four three-flat buildings had survived the bulldozer. The Tap Root Pub remained because of energetic litigation by its owner. Persons from all over Chicago put stickers on their cars reading "Save the Tap Root Pub."

This empty stretch of land was viewed by some residents of the area as a scar, the symbol of the removal of the poor and powerless. For others it stood for the promise of a stable community living in an area slightly greener, slightly more spacious than the blighted city of what is hoped to be the past. But few if any residents regarded it without some emotion. The pastor and some parishioners of the Church of the Three Crosses picked two long two-by-fours out of the rubble on Larrabee Street to fashion a cross for the church after their former cross was lost or stolen during the demonstrations in Lincoln Park in August 1968. The Reverend James Reed chose the cleared corner of Larrabee and Dickens as the site of a press conference answering charges that the North Side Cooperative Ministry had funded subversive and violent organizations.

The empty space stood for a struggle which some members of the community thought was mostly over in 1970. But it stood for struggle nonetheless. Some churches in the community took this symbol into their religious symbol system, either by making a cross or by staging a press conference, while other churches appear to have ignored it. The main concern of this study is to describe this difference in detail, and try to specify its causes.

THE FACTORY AREA

Wood-based industry moved into Lincoln Park when local timber was still available for making furniture and other wood products in the 1870s and 1880s. Because of the Chicago River, heavier industry moved in during the 1880s and 1890s. The John Deere Works of International Harvester was located in Lincoln Park until 1920. The Harvester plant relocated at that time (and the site became the CHA project known as Lathrop Homes, completed in 1938), but the area along the Chicago River in Lincoln Park is still the site of factories and warehouses. A railroad spur still in use runs through this area.

Lighter industry is also scattered through the western part of Lincoln Park (that is, from Halsted Street west). There is apparently very little social interaction between the factories and the neighborhood. Few local residents work in these factories. There is no single large employer to become a focal point of local consciousness, no single large company dominating the factory area. The physical presence of the factories rather creates socially dead space on the southwestern edge of the community.

THE MEETING PLACES OF LINCOLN PARK

There are over sixty restaurants and over forty taverns in the Lincoln Park area, there are also forty-four churches in the community. All of these, as well as some movie theatres and street corners, are in some sense meeting places.

In 1970 the ethos of this form of leisure activity had been to some extent politicized in Lincoln Park. In addition to the usual social (middle class versus working class) and cultural (artists versus business-oriented, homosexual versus heterosexual, cosmopolitan versus local) typologies, some meeting places specialized in a politically oriented clientele. One indicator of this political typology is the degree to which, in any particular pub, it is acceptable to refer to a policeman as a "pig."

The majority of the bars in the area were still meeting places for local people employed in conventional occupations who simply wanted to relax from the day's work by engaging in small talk, self-display, and sexual game-playing. They listened to radicals with interest, as they would to storytellers describing a utopian world of fantasy. Of these local bars, the ones located on commercial streets were more open to expressions of political dissent and radical philosophies than those located away from commercial streets. This is because there was more general flow of casual out-group traffic into these meeting places than into those on side streets, visited only by people who had heard about it from others.

The cosmopolitan bars were also politically neutral and open, because the ethos of the cosmopolitan meeting place is contrary to the expression of deep personal bonds such as intimacy or commitment. The cosmopolitan bar tends to cultivate civil rather than primordial ties. The sexual relationships initiated in such a setting are assumed to be casual and temporary rather than intimate and durable. The exceptions may serve to prove the rule. These bars do not so much contribute to the solidarity of a particular community as they permit their patrons to survey the beliefs and activities of communities other than their own.

But in 1970 there were some meeting places in Lincoln Park where persons went to meet others who shared deep opposition to political and cultural values of American life. These were principally the meeting places of members of the counterculture, as well as those termed "marginal." These places were only a very small percentage of the whole number of bars, taverns, and other meeting places in the area. But the fact that they existed at all was evidence of a significant change in the social structure of meeting places in the area.

All along the main streets of Lincoln Park there is plenty of activity from mid-morning to late at night. The texture of social life in and around the meeting places is rich and involved. Residents going shopping as a part of their daily lives rub shoulders with citizens of different appearance and different social philosophy. News of fights, disturbances, and police raids is not only reported by newspapers but spread rapidly by word of mouth.

The quality of life along the streets and in the bars and restaurants calls into play judgments based on subcultural fears and prejudices. The relationships here are not simply formal and commercial; whole ways of life are portrayed and placed in confrontation. The mood along Lincoln Avenue in 1970 was one of intense excitement, but also of troubled disagreement and the delicately balanced possibility of open conflict.

But there were meeting places of another kind, too, most frequently used on Sunday mornings. These were the forty-four churches of Lincoln Park. The central concern of this study is their contribution and response to the social life of the community and their impact on it.

CONCLUSION

Lincoln Park is a community of long-standing ethnic, economic, and ecological diversity. After World War II, what was once a reasonably harmonious cultural mosaic became an area of multigroup conflict. The first element of conflict was introduced by the need to remove urban blight. The process of urban renewal brought about conflict between different economic groups—institutions, real-estate speculators, and middle-class homeowners on the one hand, and the poor on the other hand. The inability of the government or society to handle the problem of urban blight except by removal of the poor was at first seen as a deficiency of the city's political structures. But as the war in Vietnam wore on and the political and cultural dissenters of the counterculture moved into Lincoln Park, these local conflicts were escalated to the level of national and international ideological conflicts. Mutually beneficial negotiations between local groups had already begun to break down in 1967, when the Reverend James Reed was removed from the Human Relations Committee of the Lincoln Park Conservation Association. The zero-sum game of community politics was only reinforced—although substantially—by the rhetoric and violence of the convention demonstrations of 1968 and by the activities of the Young Lords Organization and the Concerned Citizens Survival Front. Clergy, church congregations, and church buildings were real and symbolic participants in all stages of this escalation.

Although the original diversity of Lincoln Park made it a peculiarly fertile social field for the emergence of conflicts, it differs only in degree from many other communities and neighborhoods in major American cities. The divisions between rich and poor, ethnic majority and ethnic minorities, culture and counterculture, traditional political machine and political radicals, all exist in many other places, but Lincoln Park is one of the few places where they all exist together.

Amid these tensions and conflicts, religious ritual continues. In forty-four churches every Sunday morning, a significant minority of Lincoln Park residents come together to portray for themselves an image of the whole cosmos, to touch their concerns in everyday life to the meaning-giving symbols of religious traditions.

In their ritual, different groups of worshipers interpret their social milieu in very different ways. In order to gain a better understanding of how and why some of these ways differ, we now turn to a discussion of the churches of Lincoln Park.

CHAPTER 3

The "Dying Churches"?

The social context of the development of interaction ritual is one of widespread secular change. One symptom of the impact of such change on churches in Lincoln Park in 1965 was the use of a new phrase: "the dying churches." The vast majority of churchgoers were familiar with the phrase, and although there were different theories about the reason for the demise of the churches and different evaluations of the phenomenon, most churchgoers knew what was meant when someone spoke of "the dying churches."

The meaning of the phrase includes two forms of impending extinction of a church or congregation. One form of "dying" is essentially socioeconomic: the loss of market position of churches or decreasing memberships and revenues. The other form of dying is the apparent diminishing effectiveness of the meaning-giving function of religion, as manifested in unresolved disputes among churchgoers and the claims of ex-churchgoers that the church in general and its ritual in particular do not "do anything" for them.

Both the loss of market position and the diminishing effectiveness of religion's meaning-giving function were seen as occurring on both a national level and a local level. The interpretations of events on each level converged. That is, national trends supported interpretations of local events, and local events supported the interpretation of national trends.

It is noteworthy that participants in interaction ritual interpreted the phenomenon of "the dying churches" as an opportunity, whereas participants in mass ritual tended to fear it. One Lincoln Park pastor put it this way:

> A practical, critical thing is that when a young guy comes out, the places
> they send them to are the dying churches, either rural or city, or some-
> where in between, and of course, this is much more attractive, and it's
> much more open, with a lot of possibilities.

The reason this situation was seen as attractive and open was that it
offered the possibility of experimenting with the traditional use of
religious symbols, in order to develop new methods of performing
the meaning-giving function of religion. The pastor just quoted was
indeed hopeful that changes in church life and ritual would improve
its market position, but he was not optimistic. His view was that the
experimentation was necessary whether it enhanced the church's
market situation or not. Being in a "dying church" was therefore a
welcome opportunity, because the probability that the members of
the congregation would cooperate in experimentation was increased
by their awareness of the church's threatened extinction.

Another pastor told me of the 50 percent decrease in the size of
his congregation over the previous decade and then added, "But of
course, we are not a dying church." Although this pastor could
hardly fail to note the downward trend in membership, he did not
see any loss of validity in the doctrinal and liturgical traditions of
his church. The traditional ritual was meaningful for him and the
number of remaining members of the congregation was still sizable,
and therefore the church was not dying.

Thus it is clear that the trends and events which formed the context of the phrase "the dying churches" were open to different interpretations. There is a point of view from which the order of the
world is seen as collapsing and which therefore calls for new ways of
infusing meaning into social experience. There is also a point of view
in which the fundamental order of the world is still well served by
established ways of handling religious symbols.

THE "GENERAL MALAISE" OF THE CHURCHES

On the national level, the mid-1960s were a time of unusual crisis for
American churches. A "profound confusion and disorientation"[1]
has gripped the middle-class stratum[2] of American religious institu-

---

[1] Daniel Callahan, "Foreword," in Rosemary Haughton, *The Transformation
of Man* (Springfield, Ill.: Templegate Publishers, 1967), p. 3.

[2] The fundamentalist and pentecostal churches—the "churches of the disinherited"—did not display this same malaise. In Lincoln Park, the number of

tions since the early part of the decade. At that time the "mainline denominations" of American religion were in a new situation. As one commentator noted:

> There can no longer be any doubt that the Church has entered into a period of profound confusion and disorientation. Far from curing all our ills, the Second Vatican Council succeeded mainly in revealing how deep seated are the problems of contemporary Christianity.[3]

The essence of this confusion and disorientation was the complexity of their sources. There was no common understanding among churchmen of the causes of the crisis, but there was much agreement on its symptoms.

In the first place, there was the loss of market position of mainstream religion in America. Secondly, there were the deeply felt disputes *within* the churches about the morality of central institutions of American social and political life.

This highly generalized confusion was a condition of recent origin. In the first half of the twentieth century, the churches appeared to take for granted the task of preaching a gospel which was the continuation of ethnic traditions merging with a homogenized "American way of life." The culture religions[4] of the Old World and the American frontier were in the process of becoming the culture religions of a self-confident American synthesis.

The European immigrants to Chicago in the nineteenth and early twentieth centuries for the most part brought their churches with them. All of these older churches have undergone many vicissitudes since their establishment in the city. All have been subject to the

---

these churches increased during the sixties, and on a wide front the spokesmen for these churches could be heard saying to their middle-class sister churches: "I told you so. Your liberal secular involvement has brought you to grief." This agony and discomfort of the mainline churches vis-à-vis the continued self-assuredness of the insistently "other-worldly" fundamentalists beg for commentary. But we must leave that commentary aside until we have satisfactorily described and probed the meaning of the malaise of the churches "of the middle." The fundamentalists we shall always have with us, but the discomfort of the middle class is probably a more sensitive indicator of the central issues of social and cultural change.

[3] Callahan, p. 3.

[4] "Culture religion" is that form of religion which "does not generate its own values; instead it sanctifies the values present in the general community. There is little if any difference between the values propagated by the religious institution and those of any secular institution of equivalent status in the community" (Peter Berger, *The Noise of Solemn Assemblies* [Garden City, N.Y.: Doubleday, 1961], pp. 40–41). Berger reviews the contributions of several sociologists and anthropologists to the description and analysis of culture religion.

changes wrought by the cycle of ethnic "invasion and succession."
Some have changed according to Troeltsch's classic description of the
process of movement, from "sectlike" to "churchlike" institutions.
Until the early 1960s all of them also had a history of uninterrupted
respectability and stability as regards their place in the community.
The symbolic core of their institutional life—the structure and the
content of the worship service—had a similar history of stability and
continuity.

This certainly does not mean that ritual did not change in those
decades. In fact, the use of European languages such as German
gradually gave way to English in worship and preaching; the frontier
preference for untrained clergy gradually gave way to the calling of
men trained in college-type seminaries. But during this time, no
churches were publicly labeled as politically radical, nor were any of
their congregations stimulated to think deeply about the "relevance"
and "meaning" of their ministry. The churches seemed to be accepted and taken-for granted institutions which gave "quality and
depth to the external and social aspects of the public life of the
community."[5]

By 1965, however, this image of serene harmony between religious institutions and their secular environment had begun to fade
into a memory. Its place was taken, in the community at large, by
such phenomena as churches losing the majority of their regular
members, and a new political typology of churches. It was in the late
sixties that the first talk was heard of "radical" churches. Believers as
well as nonbelievers were faced with the issue of whether churches
are necessary to the community at all. Some people in the churches
as well as outside them were saying openly: "Maybe we can do without them."

LOSS OF MARKET POSITION

One part of the new situation is the loss of market position of religious institutions indicated by the statistical indicators of religious
belonging in the United States. Gallup polls taken through 1969
show a decline in adult attendance at Sunday worship from 49 percent of the population in 1958 to 43 percent in 1968. The Harris
polls indicate that a majority of Americans think that religion is

[5] Arthur J. Vidich and Joseph Bensman, *Small Town in Mass Society* (New
York: Doubleday Anchor Books, 1960), pp. 261, 262.

losing its influence in American life.[6] In 1970 the seventy-year trend of continuous growth of the Roman Catholic church was reversed. For the first time since 1900, it declined in numbers in every statistical category (for example: aggregate membership, number of clergy, of parishes, of seminaries and seminarians, of primary and secondary schools and pupils).[7] This reversal had been heralded by smaller annual increases, and even declines in some categories, beginning in the early sixties.

Both the clergy and the laity of the churches of Lincoln Park were aware of this general deterioration in the market position of institutional religion. They discussed it in reference to cutbacks of denominational budgets for social-service programs, the decreasing number of young people receiving the sacrament of confirmation, the vague similarity between their own use of ritual and the great attractiveness for young people of the Sunday rock concerts in Lincoln Park. Some interpreted these trends and events as "revolution," the "rise of irreligion," or a mystery that had no adequate label.

In Roman Catholic congregations, the Second Vatican Council is often referred to as the epoch-defining event that divides the present era from the past. The phrases "since Vatican Two" or "before the Council" preface statements about church decorations, Young Adult Clubs, and many other aspects of church life. But this use of the Second Vatican Council as a pervasive reference point for structuring recent history is limited to Roman Catholics. Protestants refer to it much less frequently, and when they do, they are usually talking about changes in the behavior of Catholics.

Some commentators on the new situation of the churches in Western society (not only the United States) saw this meeting of Roman Catholic bishops, which continued for four years (1962–1966), as a singularly important event contributing to recent changes.[8] But for

---

[6] For a summary of the Gallup and Harris findings, see Jeffrey K. Hadden, *The Gathering Storm in the Churches* (New York: Doubleday, 1969), pp. 15–18.

[7] For a summary of these statistics, see *The National Catholic Reporter*, May 22, 1970, p. 1.

[8] See for example, Malcolm Boyd, ed., *The Underground Church* (New York: Sheed and Ward, 1968), and Douglas Roche, "The Challenge to Authority in the Catholic Church," in *American Mosaic: Social Patterns in Religion in the United States*, ed. Philip E. Hammond and Benton Johnson (New York: Random House, 1970). Boyd attributes the impetus for the Underground Church to "the Ecumenical Movement and the dynamism of John XXIII and Vatican II" (p. 3). Roche sees Vatican Two's discussion of the nature of the church as a charter for the crises within the churches.

The Council was surely an important event, partly as symptom, partly as

the churchgoers of Lincoln Park, even for the Catholics who refer to it continually, it was only one symptomatic event among many others. They saw their new situation as part of pervasive trends that they did not understand.

INTERNAL CONFUSION

Associated with this decline in the market position of the mainline denominations were the confusions and disputes within the churches over how to respond to important social issues of American society. Jeffrey Hadden has documented this confusion with respect to the civil rights confrontations of the mid-sixties.[9] Hadden says that these demonstrations helped to reveal a threefold crisis of the churches: (1) a crisis of meaning and purpose; that is, *relevance,* (2) a crisis of belief itself, as indicated by the "death of God" theologies, and (3) a crisis of authority.

We should add that it was not only the civil rights demonstrations which were problematic for the church but also the Vietnam war, the treatment of inner-city poor, the politics of the New Left, and the life style of the counterculture. All these social, political, and cultural trends provided a dilemma for the church that struck at the very center of its function as a social institution. This function is to give meaning—that is, to provide members with a moral map of the world that enables them to distinguish good from evil. When churches can no longer perform this meaning-giving function, they are threatened not simply with a statistical death, expressed in loss of members, but with a functional death: the inability to do for society what they are supposed to do. The threat of functional death is felt most keenly by clergy and those members of the churches who take the specifically religious aspect of their institution seriously.

We should note at this point that there are four ideal responses to the threat of functional extinction. One is to give up the collective attempt to provide basic meanings and therefore to drift away from any adherence to religious symbol systems and institutions. A second

---

cause, partly as effect of more diffuse sociocultural trends. We cannot say it is the cause of some specific changes in Lincoln Park. Rather than be concerned with such "weighting" of causal factors, in this study we are concerned with the insights to be gained from a detailed analysis of local religious ritual. For such analysis, events such as the Second Vatican Council merely contribute to the general context.

[9] Hadden, p. 5ff.

is to reaffirm the certainties of traditional religious symbols and not seek to integrate new phenomena or trends. A third is to concentrate on other-worldly orientations: for example, to develop an exclusive concern for "salvation" and "union with Jesus" at the expense of extended consideration of the complexity of this-worldly moral issues. A fourth response is to take seriously the complexity of new moral issues and try to construct a religious symbol system which is faithful both to the novelty of these issues and to the presumed wisdom of traditional religion.

The responses of church members throughout America in the face of the profound social and cultural changes of the late 1960s have varied. But this diversity of response has had the effect of disrupting the calm self-confidence of mainstream institutional religion.

THE PATTERN OF DENOMINATIONAL TRADITIONS

Each of the many Christian denominations in America has its own particular set of traditions. Niebuhr's classic work *The Social Sources of Denominationalism* is still the best description of the range of those traditions. But in respect to our understanding of the phenomenon of "the dying churches," there is one distinction whose importance is greater than all others. This is the distinction between "mainline denominations" and "fundamentalist churches." This distinction is not always adequate, for there are "mainline fundamentalist churches." But the usual meaning of the distinction is of great importance.

Mainline denominations in America have generally been those churches which have taken this-worldly concerns very seriously. For such churches, a central function of dogma has been either to legitimize or to criticize the dominant social institutions of America. Fundamentalist churches, on the other hand, have restricted their central concerns to the "fundamentals" of religion, which are other-worldly in nature—salvation and damnation, union with God or Jesus, and the personal traits which are considered beneficial or detrimental with regard to an other-worldly destiny. This dominant concern for other-worldly issues tends to personalize religious morality at the expense of the morality of institutions and to flatten out the contours of the social world, leading to global condemnation or approval of this-worldly phenomena.

Thus, in the face of profound social and cultural change, mainline denominations are subject to confusion and debates which inhibit their meaning-giving function, whereas fundamentalist churches appear by contrast to be sources of greater clarity and certitude during periods of dramatic change. This is one reason why "the dying churches" in the late 1960s were those of the mainline denominations and why, at the same time that those churches felt threatened with social death, fundamentalist churches and sects such as the Jesus Freaks experienced an influx of new members.

These national trends and religious patterns are found in Lincoln Park, blended with purely local conditions which modify them and form the social context for the emergence of interaction ritual.

THE MARKET SITUATION IN LINCOLN PARK

Toward the end of 1970, there were forty-four churches or centers of popular religious activity in the Lincoln Park community area. It will be useful to group these institutions into four categories: (1) churches serving minor ethnic groups, (2) pentecostal, "fundamentalist," and Baptist churches, (3) members of the North Side Cooperative Ministry, and (4) other established churches.

The five churches for demographically small ethnic groups were two Buddhist institutions, two Korean Christian churches, and a Greek Orthodox church. The fifteen pentecostal or fundamentalist churches included the meeting hall of the Jehovah's Witnesses, some Baptist churches, and storefronts for Spanish-speaking worshipers. The thirteen member-churches of the North Side Cooperative Ministry included many of the larger and older churches in the area, both Protestant and Roman Catholic. The eleven other established churches included most of the Roman Catholic churches and the more conservative Protestant congregations. Of the four churches included in this study, two were members of the North Side Cooperative Ministry (the Church of the Three Crosses and St. Paul) and two were from the other established churches (St. James and St. Clement).

In the number and distribution of churches, Lincoln Park is a "typical" community area of Chicago. The telephone directory lists approximately 2,300 churches within the city limits. About 300 of these are Roman Catholic; Lincoln Park therefore has slightly more than the average for the city. The area is also somewhat distinctive in that it contains two of the three Buddhist houses of worship in the city, even though most of the Japanese patrons of these temples live in Lake View rather than in Lincoln Park itself.

The age of the churches in the community ranges from those founded in the 1850s (for example, St. Michael, St. Paul, and Mc-Cormick) to those founded in 1970 (two storefront churches, Iglesia de Dios and the Church of the New Truth). The majority of the churches in Lincoln Park date from the last three decades of the nineteenth century, the time when the community was reaching residential maturity. An interesting cutting point for determining the age of churches in the community is World War II. Table 3 shows the distribution that results if we list the ages of the churches by the four types mentioned above and call those "old" that were founded before World War II.

The "invasion" of the fundamentalist and pentecostal churches is more recent and more pronounced than even the cutting point of World War II might show, for nine of the twelve "new" fundamentalist churches have opened since 1960. All three of the "old" fundamentalist congregations are white; of the twelve "new" congregations, seven are predominantly white, three are black, and two are Spanish-speaking.

Another aspect of church life in the community is the type of building used by the congregations. Thirty-one centers of religious activity in Lincoln Park use church buildings—that is, buildings originally designed for worship or specifically religious activities; thirteen use "secular" buildings such as storefronts, meeting halls, or apartments. By type, this distribution is as shown in table 4.

In regard to size, the modal seating capacity of church is 400 persons. There are six very large churches in the area, with seating capacities of 1,000 persons or more.

The size of *congregations* is much harder to measure because of

TABLE 3. Ages of the Four Types of Churches, by Time of Founding

Type	"Old"	"New"	% Old
Minor Ethnic	4	1	80
Pentecostal, etc.	3	12	20
North Side Cooperative Ministry	11	2	85
Other Established	11	0	100

TABLE 4. Type of Building Used by the Congregations

Type	"Church"	"Secular"
Minor Ethnic	4	1
Pentecostal, etc.	7	8
North Side Cooperative Ministry	11	2[a]
Other Established	9	2[b]

[a]The office of the McCormick Student Body, and the Community Arts Foundation.
[b]Opus Christi and the Christian Science Reading Room.

the wide variety of record-keeping systems. From observations we can assert that an "average" congregation in Lincoln Park has about 300 members, but that the storefront-church congregations are generally much smaller than that, usually fewer than 100 members.

A few churches in Lincoln Park went out of business entirely between 1960 and 1970. One church building was torn down by urban renewal and its congregation disbanded. Another large church building was sold to developers, since it was no longer needed as the annex for the Belden Avenue Baptist Church. A third building was transferred from a mainline denomination to a fundamentalist congregation. A fourth building (Armitage Avenue Methodist) had an extremely small congregation (twelve members) and was used extensively by local community organizations as an office and meeting place.

What emerges from this summary view of religious belonging in Lincoln Park is a pattern which appears to be typical of inner-city transitional areas. The majority of the older churches are smaller than they were twenty years ago. There has been an "invasion" of fundamentalist churches, which is due to the fact that the newer ethnic groups brought their churches with them, just as the older groups had done. Fewer than 10 percent of the churches appear to be threatened with total extinction, but all mainline churches are in a state of decline.

The most clearly "dying" churches are the fewer than 10 percent whose continued physical existence is in question, but other mainline churches are affected by these few. The few cases of complete extinction are seen both against the background of a general decline in the market position of mainline denominations and also against the background of the moral and theological issues associated with such extinction. From familiarity with the reasons members leave churches, local believers know that loss of members is related to moral, religious, and ideological differences. Either the church is not speaking out on the right issues, or it is speaking out too strongly on some issues, or it is simply saying the wrong thing.

How this confusion helps to create the image of "dying churches" in Lincoln Park can be seen more clearly and concretely if we look at the history of the North Side Cooperative Ministry, a body founded as an explicit response to that phenomenon. The North Side Cooperative Ministry is an integral part of the social history of the new *political* typology of churches which emerged in Lincoln Park in the late 1960s. NSCM itself and some of its member churches were the religious groups labeled "radical" by other persons and groups within the community.

THE NORTH SIDE COOPERATIVE MINISTRY

"The North Side Cooperative Ministry was inaugurated on Palm Sunday, 1963, with fifteen churches accepting the common covenant."[10] This organization included churches from the Near North community area, Lake View, and Lincoln Park. Its founders saw themselves as members of dying churches, and they tended to view this phenomenon as occurring only in the inner city. But although they thought that the distribution of their situation was local, they viewed its meaning as universal:

> While churches in suburban areas experienced a considerable boom in institutional life in the years following World War II, many of their counterparts in the inner-city declined. This has been true on the north side of Chicago. Population shifts left many local congregations with memberships decreasing, financial support declining, and property deteriorating. Pastors have often felt lonely, unsupported, and unable to bring adequate resources to bear for effective ministries. Many of the small and medium sized churches of the mainline denominations became preoccupied with their struggle for survival. This very struggle eventually became a crucial "catalyst" for change in the life of many churches.[11]

[10] Lawrence Witmer, "Studies in Comparative Ministry for Urban Mission: The North Side Cooperative Ministry and the Christian Action Ministry in Chicago, Illinois" (mimeographed report, August 1966), p. 5. By 1967, membership had increased to twenty-six churches, half of which were located in the Lincoln Park community area.

[11] Decreasing membership, declining financial support, and the lonely, unsupported pastor are all elements of what Lifton refers to as the "coercive infallible environment" and its impact on identity. (See Robert Jay Lifton, *Thought Re-*

These churchmen thus saw themselves—in their role as churchmen —threatened with extinction by an "infallible environment," in Robert Jay Lifton's terms. But at the same time that the environment challenged the viability of their former commitments, it did not propose any new ideology to which they might convert, so as to find a new life in a new commitment. These churchmen did, however, clearly see the threat of institutional death as an invitation to seek new sources of life, as the young pastor quoted earlier (p. 40) observed.

The most immediate form of new life that these churchmen devised was simply the creation of a new organization. This organization, with its communications network, began to create a self-conscious subcommunity among the churched residents of Lincoln Park. In the absence of any viable symbols of commitment coming from secular society to which they might "convert," they turned to the symbols of Christianity and recommitted themselves to certain of those.

The NSCM had a full-time director whose principal function was to call and organize monthly meetings and an annual conference which discussed aspects of social life including eleven topical headings, plus informal seminars and work groups. In their nine-hour annual conference, about seventy-five clergy and laity from the twenty-six member-churches of the NSCM made plans for activities under the following headings: (1) Education, (2) Peace (education and action), (3) Black Power, (4) Young Adults, (5) Spanish Power, (6) Poverty Power, (7) Community Organizations, (8) Politics-Pollution, (9) Housing, (10) Health (and Mental Health), (11) Student Power. Very few of these plans were ever implemented by "task forces" of the NSCM, but the meeting served the function of creating an image of the churches' vital participation in the life of the community.

The preamble to the constitution of the North Side Cooperative Ministry begins: "We, the people of God . . . ," and this reaffirmation

---

form and the Psychology of Totalism [New York: W. W. Norton, 1961], pp. 67ff. and 438ff.) It appears that what is true of individuals is also true sometimes of groups and institutions. Physical deprivation can be a kind of psychic shock which leads to a change, or the attempt to change, a whole world view. One of Lifton's anecdotes about thought reform demonstrates the extreme form of this kind of process. ". . . the judge asked, 'Now, have you any intention of being sincere?' Father Luca replied, 'I want to be sincere and obedient, but I am not certain how to do it. I hope you will show me a way.' To which the judge answered, 'I will show you a way,' and then called in several prison guards and left the room. These newcomers proceeded . . . over the course of the night to inflict upon him a series of painful injuries, mostly to his back. When they had left him about dawn, he lay helpless . . . with multiple fractures of his vertebral column" (p. 48).

of the "great" tradition of Christianity now crossed denominational
lines. It became furthermore a guarantee of this community's continued possession of institutional life, despite the deterioration of the
churches' market situation. The North Side Cooperative Ministry's
confidence in the viability of this new community of believers expressed itself in unrealistically inflated programs of activities for its
members.[12] Along with these exaggerated symbols of new life, however, there is in the membership of the NSCM some realistic awareness also.

While the original hope of the NSCM was to build a widespread
solidarity among believers on the north side of Chicago, and thus
constitute a new and durable community, its participants recognize
that this was not achieved. The solidarity built up was among pro-
fessional churchmen and "activists." "Participants agree that the
Common Council is not truly representative of the overall constitu-
ency; delegates tend to be activists of relatively liberal social per-
suasion."[13]

In the political disputes of the community, the members of the
NSCM conceived of themselves as mediators providing a common
ground of understanding to all parties in disputes. They therefore in-
tervened in the demonstrations in Lincoln Park in August 1968 and
tried to mediate between police and demonstrators in October 1969.
Their openness to all points of view led to their being called both
"naive" and "subversive" by a segment of the community closely
connected with the Lincoln Park Conservation Association. The
events in question happened as follows.

The North Side Cooperative Ministry brought together about fifty
north side pastors and concerned churchmen in the Church of the
Three Crosses (two blocks from the park) on the evening of August
27, 1968. On this Tuesday night, a major confrontation took place

---

[12] The official report of NSCM (in 1966) lists its activities as follows: (1)
Ministry with Young Adults, (2) Ministry to the Elderly, (3) Ministry to Pre-
School Children, (4) Ministry with Cultural and Ethnic Groups, (5) Ministry for
Racial and Social Justice, (6) Ministry on Housing, (7) Ministry on Public Welfare, (8) Ministry with Community Organizations, (9) Ministry through the Arts,
(10) Ministry in Christian Education, (11) Ministry of Developing Structures
for Mission.

There is no intention in our comments here to derogate the sincerity of the
commitments to these programs, nor its subjective authenticity; but in fact the
rhetoric of these programs far exceeded performance, indicating that the central
function of the programs is a symbolic definition of institutional life and viability
rather than a pragmatic division of normal labor.

[13] Witmer, p. 21.

between Chicago police and demonstrators in Lincoln Park. When it became clear to the assembly in the Church of the Three Crosses that a violent confrontation was about to take place, they decided to take from the Church of the Three Crosses its huge cross (fourteen feet tall and made of eight-by-eight timbers), go with it to the park, and take their stand between the police lines and the demonstrators. They apparently managed to delay the clearing of the park by this move, but in the end the confrontation did take place, and the huge cross was left on the grass during the encounter. The next morning it was nowhere to be found, and the common surmise of the church members is that it was removed and destroyed by the police.[14]

In October of 1969, the Weatherman faction of the Students for a Democratic Society planned an action in Lincoln Park, and the Revolutionary Youth Movement II (RYM II) group of SDS planned a march starting at the "People's Park" in the center of the Lincoln Park community area. Prior to the actual demonstration and march, pastors of the NSCM called a meeting with city and police officials. The deputy chief of police in charge of task force, three corporation counsels, five pastors, and representatives of the Lincoln Park Conservation Association were invited and attended. Representatives of RYM II were not invited but attended anyway. The original hope of the NSCM pastors was to get the city to suspend the ordinance forbidding the use of Lincoln Park after 11:00 P.M. They thought this would help avoid the inevitable confrontation which was making this community area the "demonstration capital of the world."

The city either could not or would not suspend the ordinance, and the meeting ended with the city officials reminding the churchmen

---

[14] The multivalence and the power of this symbol is attested to by these events. The ministers took it to the park because "it was something that could be *seen* as a rallying point" and because it stood for their prophetic tradition. Some members of the congregation of the Church of the Three Crosses—who had not been consulted because the action developed spontaneously out of the assembly of churchmen and the events in the park—saw its use in this connection as a "desecration." These were principally the members of the old St. James United Church of Christ, one of the two congregations which merged to form the Church of the Three Crosses in 1965. The cross in question had been St. James's cross, and when the congregations merged, St. James's building was rented to the Old Town Players, and the building of the Second Evangelical United Church on Wisconsin and Sedgwick streets was used for worship. Thus the cross was the last remaining physical symbol of the existence of the old St. James congregation. Its loss was a final blow to some members of that church, and as a result they stopped coming to services at the Church of the Three Crosses. It is hardly probable that whoever did remove the cross from the park was unaware of its symbolic value.

of their obligation to obey the law and the churchmen reminding the police that they might have higher obligations.

Although the North Side Cooperative Ministry saw itself as an open-minded mediator, one group of citizens of Lincoln Park saw the NSCM as the enemy. This group, which called itself UPTIGHT,[15] made its first public appearance in the fall of 1969, when leaflets were passed out at the doors of several suburban churches, signed: "A grouping of people who are U.P.T.I.G.H.T., United People To Inform Good-doers Here and There." One paragraph of this leaflet states:

> The "we" of this fact sheet are not very well organized, particularly when compared to the local youth organizations that have 24 hour paid office staffs, public relations personnel, printing facilities, *free offices and head-quarters in area churches,* and small-arms arsenals.

A few months later, in the spring of 1970, members of UPTIGHT (and of the Lincoln Park Conservation Association[16]) offered their services to Senator McClelland's Senate Subcommittee on Internal Security, to testify about subversive activities in the community of Lincoln Park. Their offer was accepted, and testimony was given in Washington on August 3, 1970. The witnesses testified on the basis of their "year-long study of the various revolutionary factions in the Lincoln Park area," asserting that "the North Side Cooperative Ministry has spawned all of these children, such as the Young Lords, the Concerned Citizens Survival Front, Young Patriots Organization, and even part of La Gente. . . ."[17]

The day after the story broke, the three ministers mentioned by name in the newspaper article (they did not have transcripts of the actual testimony) held a news conference in a vacant lot on Larrabee Street (in the "disputed territory"), denied the charges made against

---

[15] Although UPTIGHT attacked the North Side Cooperative Ministry as an organization, it also focused special attention on the three "radical" Methodist churches in Lincoln Park: The Parish of the Holy Covenant (whose pastor was James Reed), the Armitage Avenue People's Church, and the Church of the Three Crosses.

[16] The connection between UPTIGHT and LPCA was unpublished public knowledge in the community until January 1970, when the *Lincoln Park Press* (Prensa) published the names of eleven members of UPTIGHT. Six of these were members of the board of LPCA.

[17] *Chicago Daily News,* January 17, 1971. The testimony was not made public until this date. The two witnesses who appeared before the subcommittee were Harry Port of UPTIGHT and LPCA, and Hugh Patrick Feely, executive director of LPCA.

them, and explained their position on the local issues mentioned in the testimony.

In mid-1971, this conflict was still going on. Members of UPTIGHT informed members of the "radical" churches that they had "done their homework" and would indeed remove the pastors and members of these churches from positions of influence in the various community organizations in Lincoln Park, and would eventually remove these churches from the community by cutting off their financial support.[18]

SUMMARY

By the mid-1960s, the context for the religious ritual of middle-class religion was no longer a comfortable harmony between religion and ethnic groups becoming assimilated to a self-confident American society. For reasons as yet unanalyzed, a general malaise had gripped the mainline denominations—a confusion and disorientation which sought "meaning" and "relevance" in an unprecedented way.

In the community of Lincoln Park, the generalized frustration of the churches was augmented by the existence of "the dying churches" —churches which appeared to be losing their social existence as a result of a combination of local ecological patterns (the movement of older ethnic groups to the outer city and the suburbs) and the deterioration of institutional religion's market position on a national scale. Along with this loss of certainty about their position in the community, the churches were called upon to respond to a new definition of local political life, one which included the escalation of local conflicts to an ideological dimension with deeply moral connotations. The churches were therefore entering an uncharted area in which they had widely divergent alternatives from which to choose an interpretation of the meaning of the world in which they found themselves.

The principal device by which the Christian religion defines the

[18] UPTIGHT had little success in this regard with the ecclesiastical superiors of the Methodist churches. The Northeast Illinois Conference of the United Methodist Church sponsored a procession and celebration to "reaffirm the ministry of the Methodist churches in Lincoln Park." This event took place on June 13, 1971. It consisted of a procession along Larrabee Street, from Chicago Avenue (800 N) through the Cabrini-Green Homes area, to the disputed territory. At the corner of Wisconsin and Larrabee, the participants conducted their ritual of reaffirmation.

meaning it gives to the world is the symbol system expressed in Sunday morning worship services. The churches of Lincoln Park used their worship services in different ways. Most of them continued the practice of mass ritual. But a few of them developed a kind of ritual which may be characteristic of times and places of anomie. This is the kind of ritual I have called interaction ritual.

Of the four congregations I studied closely, one made a clear choice for the development of interaction ritual. At least two other congregations among the forty-four in the area also did this. Another of my subject-congregations experimented indecisively with interaction ritual for about a year, but mass ritual continued to hold a central place there. The other two churches of the four made no moves in the direction of interaction ritual.

CHAPTER 4

Tradition and Crisis: Four Case Histories

An important problem for the sociology of religion in the context of community studies is the influence of churches in secular affairs. One of the primary interests of this focus is the stratum alignment of churches, and the manner in which such alignment affects institutional religion and its interaction with community life. Lloyd Warner used this perspective in the Yankee City series, and Liston Pope used it for *Millhands and Preachers.*

Here we want to look at churches in a community from a different perspective. Granted that churches frequently take sides in political conflicts on the basis of their alignment with certain classes, strata, or ethnic groups in a given community, "taking sides" is not the churches' basic function in the community. Taking sides in sociopolitical conflicts is rooted in complex traditions, some of which are always specifically religious. The existence of churches as ritual-performing groups is logically prior to their participation in political conflict. They *worship* together. It is because worship tends to be class-based that the political alignments of churches tend to be class-based. But as soon as we say that people go to church for worship and ritual (although there are other reasons, too), we must wonder what place in community life this worship has. The basic task of religion is a "meaning-giving" function, "placing a technical fact in the moral order,"[1] as Meyer Fortes put it.

[1] Meyer Fortes, "Ritual and Office in Tribal Society," in *Essays on Ritual and Social Relations,* ed. Max Gluckman (Manchester: Manchester University Press, 1962), p. 81.

If churches did not perform ritual, they might well remain distinctive associations in any community, but they would then become social-service agencies, political lobbies, neighborhood organizations. They would lose their specifically religious function of giving global meaning, of relating social life to ultimate meanings.

Thus, to begin to understand the place of religion in social life, we must closely examine traditions which form the context of the ritual churches perform. We know of politically involved churches and politically withdrawn ones, but we know of no churches which do not perform ritual.[2]

We must delve into the historical and social profiles of these churches, because the tendency of ritual is to be all-inclusive. That is, it tends to pick its symbolic elements from all aspects of the participants' lives. Even though we cannot specify all the distinctive characteristics of each congregation, we can press on in that direction and describe the details which give us some insight into the differences in ritual and the significance of those differences for understanding the place of religion in community life.

All four of the churches we have chosen for detailed examination are "middle class" and predominantly white. But they vary widely on other important characteristics. The Church of the Three Crosses[3] is small (96 members), of moderate income, and has a reputation for being innovative and even "radical." St. Paul United Church of Christ is large (over 1,000 members), relatively wealthy, and has a reputation for being moderate and "liberal" in religious and political affairs. St. Clement Roman Catholic Church (the only Catholic church of the four) has a congregation of over 2,000 members and a reputation for being politically conservative. St. James Lutheran Church is medium-sized (about 500 members), is of modest financial image, and has a reputation for being inactive in political affairs and very conservative in religious affairs. It is a member-church of the Missouri Synod.

[2] Even the symbolically austere meetings of the Quakers are a handling of meaning-giving process and symbols. The Quakers perhaps more than any other Western religion look for the emergence of ultimate meaning from the personal consciousness of the members of the group; but it is still ultimate meaning and moral order which their meetings seek to express. And the process by which the Quakers educe these meanings is precisely if informally prescribed.

[3] Since the name of one of the four churches is an integral part of its symbolic structure, and since all four churches must be dealt with very concretely, it is impossible to preserve the "anonymity" of these churches by using fictitious names. In citing interviews with their pastors and members, however, I have concealed all personal identities by means of coded or general references or fictitious names.

Both the Church of the Three Crosses and St. Paul are member-churches of the United Church of Christ, and both are also members of the North Side Cooperative Ministry. (The Church of the Three Crosses also sends delegates to the Northeast Illinois Conference of the United Methodist Church, and this is in fact its stronger affiliation.) All four churches have been in Lincoln Park for at least sixty-five years.[4]

THE CHURCH OF THE THREE CROSSES

The Church of the Three Crosses is a product of an involved process of fission and fusion which began in the late eighteenth century in Maryland and continued to at least 1968. The first fission was the breaking away of frontier rural churches from urban churches around 1775. Two of these new churches serving the farmers and small-town people of German ancestry were the United Brethren and the so-called Albright's People (the Evangelical Church).[5]

The United Brethren was started by a German Reformed Church minister, Philip William Otterbein, and Martin Boehm, a Mennonite pastor at odds with his church because of his revivalistic preaching. Otterbein and Boehm began their preaching in the late eighteenth century in Maryland and "Pennsylvania Dutch" country but only joined together to form the United Brethren in 1800.

The Evangelical Church also grew up among rural people of German ancestry but began with the preaching of Jacob Albright, a Methodist layman who became an itinerant preacher in 1791 at the age of thirty-two.

Both of these denominations started as itinerant preaching to rural Germans and regularly called to the ministry unschooled small-town men with the capacity for charismatic preaching. As the Germans moved west and became assimilated to some aspects of North America, English came to be used in their churches, but these still tended to be the churches of unsophisticated rural and small-town communities. It was only in the first quarter of the twentieth century that seminary-trained ministers became a respectable institution for the Evangelicals and the United Brethren. By the mid-twentieth

[4] St. Clement was founded in 1905, St. James in 1869, the Church of the Three Crosses (as Second Evangelical United Brethren Church) in 1840, and St. Paul in 1854.

[5] Paul H. Eller, *These Evangelical United Brethren* (Dayton, Ohio: Otterbein Press, 1950), *passim.*

century, the ministers of both these denominations regularly went to Bible colleges, as is the general custom in all mainline denominations in the United States.

Both the Evangelical Church and the United Brethren arose from the preaching of the Great Awakening, a movement strongly influenced by the Methodists and the Wesleyan movement. They were long separated from the main Wesleyan churches by their German (rather than English) ancestry, and from one another by devotion to different founders and minor organizational differences. The two groups finally rationalized their similarities in 1946, when they merged to form the Evangelical United Brethren Church.

The Church of the Three Crosses was originally of the Albright following. When founded in 1840, it was called the Evangelical Church and was located at Wabash and Monroe streets in what is now Chicago's central business district.[6] In 1853 the Evangelical Church divided into two congregations. One moved to a site on Clark Street near Polk (just south of "the Loop" in what is now railroad yards) and was called First Evangelical Church. The other part of the congregation built a church on the corner of Clark and Chicago (north of the Loop) and was called Second Evangelical Church. In 1869 this second church moved to its present site at the corner of Wisconsin and Sedgwick streets, in the northeast quadrant of what is now Lincoln Park. The building on this site was burned down on two occasions: first during the Great Fire of 1871 and then in 1936. The present building—still looking like "the little country church in the city"—was completed in March 1937.

The Second Evangelical Church became the Second Evangelical United Brethren Church ("Second EUB" for short) in 1946. In 1965 Second EUB began discussions with a nearby United Church of Christ (St. James, on North Park Street in Old Town) which had fallen on hard times (decreasing membership, plus the loss of a full-time pastor). Out of the merger discussions, the two congregations agreed to call the new entity the Church of the Three Crosses. The new congregation affiliated with the United Church of Christ and the Evangelical United Brethren. In 1968 the EUBs merged with the Methodist Church, giving rise to the congregation's present affiliation with the United Methodist Church.[7]

[6] John G. Schwab, *The History of the Illinois Conference of the Evangelical Church* (Harrisburg, Pa.: Evangelical Press, 1937).

[7] As mentioned above, the Methodist affiliation is taken much more seriously than that with the United Church of Christ, as the pastors of Three Crosses since the merger have been trained at the EUB seminary in Naperville, Illinois.

The congregation of the Church of the Three Crosses has always been small. When it moved to North Town in 1869, it had 70 members. It was largest in 1936, with 162 members. In 1965 its membership was 145. In 1970 it had 93 members.

The ethnic tradition of the Evangelical Church sustained the use of the German language until 1917. At that time, the historian of the Second EUB notes, "all Sunday evening services held in English." The pastor in the Evangelical tradition was called (and therefore hired) by the congregation but, once installed, was head of the congregation. He had full authority, especially in "matters of liturgy."[8] In the late 1950s and early 1960s Second EUB and St. James United Church of Christ shared a musical tradition which was further evidence of their assimilation to a middle-class style of worship. This was the tradition of using soloists and Renaissance church music (choral pieces and organ solos) as a means of enhancing a formerly plain musical format of ritual.

The general image of this Evangelical (to some extent Wesleyan) tradition is of a community of German ethnic origin and lower-middle-class rural and small-town socioeconomic condition, gradually becoming assimilated to an English-speaking, urbanizing, industrializing, stable society. From the beginning of the twentieth century until the 1960s, the hierarchical structure of the denomination, the hierarchical structures within the congregations, and the form and content of ritual all remained stable. Congregations remained small, and church buildings remained modest in size and decoration. Pastors continued to be chosen by their congregations and retained their monarchical positions within congregations once chosen.

All these elements of stability began to change dramatically in the mid-1960s. The changes which occurred before that time—the disappearance of elements of German ethnicity and frontier educational perspectives—are aspects of social and cultural assimilation to a society and a culture whose basic structure the members of this church accepted as valid and stable. This perspective of gradual upward social mobility, assimilation, and optimism is reflected in one pastor's comments on the ethos of the denomination in the late 1950s:

> We were coming out of the fifties to the high point of religious attendance and all that stuff, and I think that on our part there was a certain

---

[8] The Evangelical tradition of depending on itinerant preachers is reflected in the relatively short tenure of pastors of Second EUB. The church had thirty-six pastors in the hundred years between 1869 and 1970. This is in sharp contrast to the five to seven pastors in the same period of time in the other three churches.

rebellion against that. That's not really what the theology we believe in speaks about . . . and so we don't want to commit ourselves to big buildings, and congregations that don't understand the services. I would say the servant concept is trying to make . . . to create the matter of commitment as lying with the people, as opposed to being just a social kind of thing, which the church is of course strong on.

The congregation's understanding of the minister's role was also very clear:

> The congregation when we came here was much more conservative, a congregation of people who used to live here but had moved out . . . they were very much more traditional-minded . . . wanted pastors to bless the family, visit in their home, conduct a nice worship service on Sunday morning, take care of the church school . . . typical kind of program. That's what their orientations were. And we who were meeting in the council and so on began, through study groups, to suggest that the church is more and ought to be more than that.

The "more than that" of the new pastors was summarized in such phrases as "involvement with the community" and "dealing seriously with the question of the city." The concrete expressions of these formulas were social and political activities which frequently involved criticism of official programs.

The strains created by the difference between old and new styles of religious expression are shown in the history of the Church of the Three Crosses' association with Spanish-speaking believers. The efforts to maintain a close fit between the symbols and meanings expressed in religious ritual and a secular milieu undergoing rapid change created a split between the two groups.

From 1956 until 1968 a Spanish-speaking congregation shared the Church of the Three Crosses building with its predominantly white congregation. Although the English and Spanish worship services were usually separate, the two groups did worship together four or five times a year and considered themselves parts of the same congregation. The Spanish-speaking congregation left the Church of the Three Crosses in 1968, partly because of migration and partly because the changes taking place in the English-speaking congregation were disturbing to the more conservative of the Spanish-speaking worshipers. For example, the "secular reading" in ritual was added to the English worship service, in July 1966, but was omitted when the Spanish congregation joined the English congregation for joint worship. One pastor comments:

> I would imagine that's intentional . . . the Spanish congregation was not ready to be concerned outside its devotional and cultural life, you know, as Spanish people. And it came together for that closeness, and it did not

want to be concerned with the problems, with the rest of the community
around the neighborhood. It wanted to kind of escape from all that. . . .
This was the moment, the time to get away from all those problems, and
so as one of the Spanish laymen said, "We want to come in and pray with
our eyes closed and our head down, not have to look at all this around us."
They were isolated and certainly not feeling that they were responsible
for or had to worry on Sunday about the world around them.

When the pastors and the congregation of the Church of the Three
Crosses spoke out on such issues as the reappointment of Superintendent of Public Schools Benjamin Willis[9] and the struggles over
urban renewal, and when they moreover brought these concerns into
the sermon and other elements of ritual as well, a situation was created which could not be handled by the traditional style of religious
congregations. This style contained one specific social taboo, revealed in an interview with a pastor of the Church of the Three
Crosses.

Q: Suppose you gave a sermon on civil rights and people say it is too strong.
When you go around to people individually, does real argument go on? Is
there personal confrontation?
A: In a traditional setting it's much more difficult to bring it out honestly. If
you irritate people enough, they start talking about quitting because they're
angry. . . .
Q: But why should there be so much difficulty with honesty?
A: Well, the church has trained that out of people. One thing the church has
taught is that you love everybody, that you have good relationships with
everybody, and differences of opinion, in this view, is just not where God
is. God is in the midst of nice, loving people.
    . . . Church people don't argue. All the disagreement has to take place
outside the meetings, in rump sessions. It's not honorable to disagree in
board meetings, or a committee . . . or much less in a Sunday morning service. That's why when disturbances occur, the bishop has to call in the police
and get them out of there. If you dare to try to interrupt the drama of the
Eucharist in a Catholic church, for instance, gee, all hell would break loose.[10]

In the absence of an ethos which permits social criticism and dispute, church activities had a tendency to be concerned with social
trivia:

    In our discussions a big thing that came up a number of times was,
    "We don't want to have church meetings. We've had our fill of church

---

[9] In 1965 Superintendent Willis was much criticized by black community
groups in Chicago for not instituting the broad reforms recommended by two
separate studies done by University of Chicago sociologists in the early sixties.
These groups campaigned to prevent his reappointment by the Chicago School
Board.

[10] This interview took place shortly after the police had in fact been called
in to remove Catholic protesters from a church in Cleveland, Ohio.

meetings. We want any meetings that this church has to be significant, meetings that are dealing with important things in our lives. . . ." They're talking about committee meetings where you come in, sit down, and spend an hour and a half talking about what time the meeting is going to start and who's going to bring what for potluck.

The detachment of church life and religious ritual from a problematic social milieu is further indicated by the custom among churchgoers of returning to the church they grew up in even after they have moved out of its natural territory: "This was an old neighborhood church. A lot of them had met here when they were younger. But they were coming back now, and twenty years later they were still coming back." In this situation—where the ethical order of society is taken for granted—sermons are concerned with theological generalities or abstractions or the inculcation of the conventional personal virtues of the socioeconomic class or subculture with which the congregation identifies.

This detachment began to change in the early 1960s. The pastor of Second EUB from 1961 to 1965 began to call the congregation's attention to its secular surroundings: "But he kept bringing that whole community back to the pulpit and to the Council and started forcing them to deal with that." Because of this pressure from the previous pastor, when the new pastors arrived in 1965 "some people were on the point of leaving" the congregation and "were somehow kind of just testing out where and waiting to see where we were going to be, I think."

Thus, in the mid-sixties, this congregation began to split over what its members regarded as "stylistic" elements. Those who left complained about various apparently random elements of the church's new style, ranging from the use of banners to decorate the church to the lack of a youth program. This preference for the "old" style versus the "new" is reputed to have a correlation with age, people over fifty favoring the old style. But this correlation was not highly significant in the Church of the Three Crosses. Some older people did leave, but many stayed. Six of the forty-five most active members of the congregation were over fifty years old in 1970. Younger people also left, and the Spanish-speaking congregation departed en masse.

In terms of occupational patterns, the Church of the Three Crosses is most interesting. I could not obtain occupational data for the congregation in 1965, but in 1970 more than 40 percent of the nucleus of the congregation were employed in "interpersonal or community service" occupations as teachers, social workers, and community organizers. (Twenty of the forty-five most active members were in these occupations. This group included, besides the pastors, four ex-clergymen.) There were only two men with "business" occupations in this congregation between 1965 and 1970.

The historical social profile of the Church of the Three Crosses is essential for understanding changes in its ritual. The context of ritual tends to be the total social field of its participants' experience, and this includes its history as a lower-middle-class denomination, as well as the personalities of its pastors, its move toward concern for the city and the community, and the kinds of occupations its members hold.

In the mid-1960s the Church of the Three Crosses not only was aware of a "general malaise" affecting institutional religion in America; it was also making conscious and continuous efforts to move away from a style of religious belonging and practice which it considered "traditional" and toward a style which could be characterized only in the most general terms as one of "involvement." In short, it sought to create a church "where commitment lies with the people." This movement was seen as a new direction, a cessation of the process of assimilation and detachment from specific group concern for the ethics of the social order, which had been continuous in the church and in the denomination from its origins until the early 1960s.

ST. PAUL UNITED CHURCH OF CHRIST

Less than a mile from the Church of the Three Crosses stands St. Paul church, at the corner of Fullerton Avenue and Orchard Street, about thirty yards from the central intersection of the Lincoln Park community area. On a sign outside of the building it is called a "United Church of Christ." On the Sunday bulletin giving the order of ritual, it is called "Evangelical and Reformed." In the congregation's bylaws it is called "First Evangelical Lutheran St. Paul's Church of Chicago." This triple title arises from a process of fission and fusion similar to that which gave rise to the merged congregation of the Church of the Three Crosses.

"Old St. Paul" was founded in 1843. The first building was on a site "at the edge of town," on the corner of Ohio and LaSalle streets. The congregation was made up of recent German immigrants who still looked to "the Fatherland" for their religious traditions. "As was the custom in the Fatherland, a *Kirchenrat* (Church Council) was selected from among those present. . . ."[11]

St. Paul was thus founded by members of the established church in Germany, a church which in the nineteenth century had Zwinglian as well as Lutheran ancestry. It was the product of a state-directed merger of Lutheran and Reformed (Zwinglian) churches by Kaiser Wilhelm.

In 1846 St. Paul became one of the sites for the creation of the Missouri Synod of the Lutheran Church in America.[12] Its pastor at that time was one Augustus Selle:

> Pastor Selle had been elected as the leader on the assumption that he was an Evangelical Lutheran Pastor of the same doctrinal confession as were the pastors and churches of the Fatherland. Meanwhile, a new brand of Lutheranism had been generated in the spiritually productive religious soil of the new land. . . . Their headquarters were at St. Louis, Missouri. The Pastor was caught in the dragnet of their new Lutheran denomination, which adopted even some of the Catholic rules, i.e., private confession, the observance of new rituals in the worship and other heretofore unknown church policy in the administration of the church.[13]

The majority of the congregation of St. Paul would not accept "these innovations which were unknown to them in Germany,"[14] and so Pastor Selle and a minority of the congregation left to form Second St. Paul Church, the first Missouri Synod Congregation in Illinois.[15]

By 1850, the rapid growth of Chicago had made the original site of the church undesirable. Many members of the congregation now lived in North Town, and so "the first brick church on the north

[11] *Souvenir Book of the 96th Anniversary of St. Paul's Evangelical Lutheran Church* (Chicago: n.p., December 1938), p. 3.

[12] One historian describes the origins of the Missouri Synod thus: "Meanwhile, the conservatives were busy organizing their own synods, on the triple basis of doctrinal fidelity to the Lutheran symbols, territorial limitation, and usually a common European background. In 1847 a group of Saxon immigrants, led by Carl Walther, organized the Missouri Synod. They had come to America because of their religious convictions, to escape the Prussian Government's imposition of the union of the Lutheran and Reformed churches" (John A. Hardon, *The Protestant Churches of America* [Westminister, Md.: Newman Press, 1956], pp. 128–29).

[13] *Souvenir Book of St. Paul's,* p. 3.

[14] Ibid., p. 6.

[15] "Second St. Paul" in the history of St. Paul is called "First St. Paul" by the historian of St. James Missouri Synod Lutheran Church in Lincoln Park. Some status issues connected with this nineteenth-century fission are still unresolved.

side" was erected on the present site of St. Paul in 1854. This building burned down in the Great Fire of 1871, but the "wealthiest congregation in Chicago" was quick to rebuild the church in two years.
It is a tribute to the longstanding affluence of the congregation that
the old foundation was large enough to be the base of the new building. An important part of the new structure was one of the largest
pipe organs in the Midwest, built by Steel and Turner of Westfield,
Massachusetts.[16]

This building was destroyed by fire in 1955, but the congregation
was still prosperous enough to construct its present building on the
site of the old one by 1959.

In 1957 St. Paul—following the traditions of this theologically
more liberal wing of Lutheranism—became part of the United Church
of Christ. This denomination resulted from the national merger of
the Evangelical and Reformed churches on the one hand and the
Congregational Christian Church on the other.

Throughout its history, St. Paul has had close religious and cultural
ties with Germany. This tradition includes a serious investment in
forms of "high" culture, such as classical secular and religious music.
Public organ recitals and concerts by groups such as the Stuttgart
Brass Choir and the Dresden Boys' Choir are regular features of St.
Paul's annual programs. The *Church Quarterly* was written in German until 1928, and St. Paul still has a German-language worship
service before its English service each Sunday.

Although St. Paul preferred an emphasis on the simpler ("low
church") ritual forms of Reformed Lutheranism over the "high
church" orientation of the Missouri Synod, its general affluence
made the congregation a center of an elaborate cultural life in Lincoln Park. Over this complex of religious, cultural, and social activity
presides a pastor who usually retains his position for life. In the 128
years of its duration, St. Paul has had only eight pastors.[17] Whereas
this tradition places great emphasis on preaching—prior to 1955, the
pulpit was the geometric and symbolic center of the worship space—
it differs from the traditions of the Church of the Three Crosses in
that it tends to require that preachers "have a pulpit," a stable place
of responsibility, rather than be itinerants.

In keeping with its place as a center of (ethnic) community life,
St. Paul has developed a very large physical plant. Besides the church

[16] *Souvenir Book of St. Paul's,* p. 15.

[17] Compare this with the thirty-six pastors of the Church of the Three Crosses
during the same period.

in Lincoln Park, it administers a children's home, built in 1928, and an old people's home, opened in 1921. The life of the congregation is also carried on in numerous issue-specific organizations. In 1933, there were twenty-two such issue-specific organizations; in 1970, there were eleven.[18] Those currently active are the Daughters of Ruth (girls' Sunday School), the Dorcas Society (support of foreign and home missions), Frauenverein (church decoration), Men's Club, Mothers' Club, Sunshine Club (for working women, to visit shut-ins), Tuesday Nighters, Ushers' Association, Women's Guild, Youth Fellowship, and St. Paul's Choir.[19] Two "committees" also exist, the Christian Education Committee and the Worship and Sacrament Committee. Both of these committees became, in different ways, communications centers for members of the congregation who wished to change from old, traditional styles of worship and congregational life to new styles.[20]

About 30 percent of the most active members of the congregation of St. Paul (that is, members of the Session, or governing body) are involved in "interpersonal service occupations" (mostly teachers), but another 30 percent of the most active members are "business" occupations (e.g., corporate executives, salesmen, real-estate brokers). Another distinctive feature of St. Paul's Session is that almost half of its 180 members are over fifty years old.

Although St. Paul's congregation of over a thousand members was becoming widely dispersed after World War II, still by 1965 it had no sense of impending crisis or need for a new direction. Services were still fairly well attended (by more than 300 every Sunday), although older members commented on the vast difference in the size of confirmation classes (about 400 back in the twenties and about 15 to 20 in the sixties). Large numbers of people came back to St. Paul from their new suburban homes, especially for the service held on

[18] Many of these organizations are looked on by younger members of the congregation as old folks' social gatherings, and the center of lay activity in this congregation appears to be shifting from the more traditional clubs to the new (since 1968) committees.

[19] Until 1969, the nucleus of the choir received a salary, and the soloists who performed on Sunday were frequently not members of the congregation. The paid choir and soloists were discontinued in 1970. The church still pays an organist and a music director.

[20] Both of these committees are extremely important developments sociologically. The Worship and Sacrament Committee was regrouped in 1969 to innovate in matters of ritual and in its first eighteen months of existence failed to do so effectively. The Christian Education Committee began to innovate in early 1971. Both of these developments are discussed in more detail in chapter 6.

the last Sunday of the liturgical year—the last Sunday after Pentecost, usually in mid-November. This is called Memorial Sunday and is a ritual of remembering deceased members of the congregation. St. Paul is thus a pilgrimage church. Some make the pilgrimage annually, some three times a year, and a few more often than that.

The pastor's role in St. Paul is a focal point of the congregation's imagery of tradition. The term *Herr Pastor* comes easily to the lips of the church's members. If they are "liberal" and innovative, they use the term pejoratively; if they are conservative, they use it approvingly. But all are aware that the traditional role of the pastor in this church is a lively concern to all its members.

In St. Paul's customs, the pastor is called by the congregation, as he is in the Church of the Three Crosses. And, once called, he works with a Session of about 200 church members and a twelve-man[21] executive body (called the Church Council). But the pastor is the chief executive of the manifold activities of the congregation, and he customarily retains his office for life, thus establishing many of the ambivalences of a father-child relationship with his congregation. In matters of liturgy his authority is especially inviolate. Although he must be a good administrator, lay persons feel free to advise him in secular matters. As regards his principal function—to preach the gospel and construct the worship service—lay advice was nonexistent until very recently. He is the expert who "manipulates the symbols of the sacred."

Within its denomination, the position of St. Paul as a local congregation is one of great autonomy. Thus, many of St. Paul's ritual traditions are quite consciously its own rather than those of the denomination. Although these customs fall within the general tradition of Reformed Lutheranism, they contain conscious variations instituted by individual pastors responding to purely local conditions.

A new pastor came to St. Paul in 1963. His definitions of "authenticity" and "involvement" were couched more in theological and cultural terms (he had spent some time as an assistant pastor in Germany) than in terms expressing the relationship of the congregation to its changing social environment. St. Paul had always been "involved" in its local community in the sense of being a center of Lincoln Park's cultural as well as religious life. This involvement was expressed in the use of the large physical plant for various community programs,

---

[21] In January 1971, the first woman in St. Paul's history was elected to the Church Council. The event was noted with a high degree of consciousness by the pastor and the congregation.

such as day care for children, a church school, and meetings of community groups. St. Paul also had a record of substantial contributions to liberal church and community groups, including the North Side Cooperative Ministry and the Neighborhood Commons Association. But as regards the dimension of involvement which means making a religious-ethical judgment on specific social or political trends in the community, St. Paul under its new pastor maintained its traditional detachment. Even in 1970, a young associate pastor of St. Paul could say:

> We really cannot get into the issue of whether to pull lever IA or IB on a voting machine. That would be an illegitimate attempt to impose the pastor's views on the congregation. What we deal with is the word of justice, and leave the application and interpretation to individual members of the congregation.

And then the speaker added thoughtfully, after a pause: "But, well, sometimes the difference between lever IA and IB is considerable. I guess we should get into that. . . ."

The new pastor of St. Paul maintained continuity with the traditional view that the liturgy belongs to the pastor. "In matters of liturgy, up until very recent times, the pastor is pope." What happened in "very recent times" is the subject of the next chapter of this book; the point here is that whatever changes have occurred have grown more out of the concerns of lay and younger members of the congregation than out of the image of ritual brought to St. Paul by its pastor. The pastor and the majority of the congregation adhere to the view that the construction of ritual is the responsibility of an ordained clergyman:

> . . . the vows of ordination in our tradition hold high the presence of the word in the service, and the interpretation of the word, that his is a peculiar task for which members of the church are set apart to work at very hard. And so that interpretive task, the task of preaching, this is something that a pastor and a congregation . . . we work very hard at.

The way in which the pastor and the congregation work together is by the pastor's taking the initiative to explain to the people what the proper and authentic form of ritual is in the light of theological perspectives obtained in seminary training:

> We have tried to explain what is occurring in the flow of the liturgy, why a section of the liturgy comes at this point and not at another point. We have tried in printed matter and in discussion to make this clear. This is not something which has been interpreted necessarily well to the people and which is in a sense authentic of where the people are. This is one of

the disturbing factors of our liturgical form, and one of the problems you get in a tradition such as ours, where for thirty years the people may do something one way, and then with a change of ministers . . . a new element may come in.

Previous to the summer of 1968, the principal "new element" which entered St. Paul's ritual—and which was a subject of controversy—was what is known as the "confession and absolution." Its novelty was that it came from a "high church" tradition rather than from the "low church" tradition which St. Paul's congregation had held to under previous pastors. Although this element of ritual is today accepted by the congregation, the controversy was significant and led to having two English services every Sunday, one with a "confession and absolution" and one without.

The demonstrations in Lincoln Park during the summer of 1968, on the occasion of the Democratic National Convention, were the first events to disturb this congregation's confident adherence to traditional forms of ritual. It may seem a long distance from the yippies in Lincoln Park to the form of Sunday morning worship service in an affluent Protestant church, but the demonstrations opened a Pandora's box of conflicting opinions and beliefs, the existence of which the congregation had apparently not suspected before. That the discovery of deeply felt difference occurred so quickly and so late in the congregation's history is an interesting puzzle.

Two events drew St. Paul into the convention demonstrations. The first was the pastor's decision to allow some of the young people from out of town to sleep in the church gym during their stay in the city. The second was a sermon given by an associate pastor on the Sunday following the demonstrations, a sermon which he entitled "The Keystone Cops." The youngsters' use of the church building and the criticism of the police from the pulpit both gave rise to intense feelings. Some members of the congregation walked angrily out of church during the sermon and subsequently quit the congregation.

These breaches stimulated intensive discussion. One result was a new mandate to the Worship and Sacrament Committee to devise an experimental ritual more attractive to young people interested in "more informal" styles of worship. The activities of this committee will be discussed in more detail in chapter 6; it is clear that it was asked to respond to the revelation of fissions in the congregation brought about by the difference in attitudes toward the convention demonstrations. Before 1968 this affluent congregation conducted its worship on the assumption of homogeneity in members' beliefs and convictions. This assumed homogeneity dissolved under the impact of a political event: the convention demonstrations. From security in its possession of denominational cultural traditions, the congregation moved to awareness of a need to work out common symbols.

The old style of St. Paul was "authentic" in its own way: "The present eleven o'clock service is also authentic in terms of expressing where those people have grown from." "Where they had grown from" was the understanding of religion and its place in community life expressed in the building of the new church in 1955–1959:

> I think that the architecture here at St. Paul's reflects a very Roman understanding of the church. And the fact that the chancel is lifted up to another level above the people reflects something of that understanding of the priest, the one who intercedes on behalf of the people, or, in our terminology, the *Herr Pastor* image of the minister.

Not only was the pastor set apart from the congregation; the ritual was set apart from the ethical order of everyday life. As a group, the congregation of St. Paul did not habitually touch the reality of everyday life against the reality of the cosmic order displayed in ritual. The ritual simply displayed that (sacred) order of the cosmos—the order of "justice"—and left the making of connections between this order and social reality to individual interpretations.

These separations between pastor and congregation and between the content of ritual and the content of everyday life are but two of a number of separations that we shall examine in the following chapter. One measure of the changes occurring in religious symbol systems in contemporary life is the pressure to dissolve such separations and the pressures felt by some churches to defend them. In the case of rituals such as that of St. Paul, the church service "abandoned a portion of reality."[22] For scholars such as Herbert Fingarette, this is part of a larger syndrome:

> In the defensive response, the breakdown of ego functions (anxiety) is met with a denial of or a surrendering of some portion of those ego powers. Always surrendered to some extent is the sovereignty of the synthetic powers of the ego. Such surrender always involves the abandonment of a portion of reality. . . . It tends to increase automatic, involuntary response. Such more or less radical devices protect (at least temporarily) the remainder of the ego. . . . In the alternative case, the disintegration of ego

[22] Herbert Fingarette, *The Self in Transformation* (New York: Basic Books, 1963), p. 94.

functions is met with reparative efforts. The person grapples with the reality situation.[23]

In 1968 the congregation of St. Paul was confronted with the task of mobilizing the "synthetic powers" of the ego of the group in order to integrate portions of reality to which its common symbols and its corporate personality had not previously paid attention.

ST. CLEMENT ROMAN CATHOLIC PARISH

St. Clement is the youngest of the five Roman Catholic churches in Lincoln Park. It was founded in 1905 as a response to the increasing density of the Catholic German population of the area. Previous to this time, St. Michael (founded in 1852) and St. Teresa (founded in 1870) had been adequate for the needs of German-speaking Catholics. St. Vincent church had traditionally served the Irish and St. Josaphat served the Polish-speaking Catholics.

St. Clement was therefore founded as a bilingual "national" parish. That is, its territory covered the same territory as St. Vincent and St. Josaphat but included only the German-speaking population of that territory. By 1916, the need for a "national" parish in this area had so decreased that St. Clement was changed to a regular territorial parish, as is the usual form of organization in the Roman Catholic church. By 1916, then, it was serving all Catholics in the northeast quadrant of Lincoln Park. The Catholics of St. Clement first built a primary school and held Mass in the hall of that building until 1918, when the present Byzantine-style church building was completed.

Like the Protestant churches in this part of Lincoln Park, St. Clement originally served a wealthy and stable population. But the strongest element of tradition affecting the organization and ritual of St. Clement is its place in the Roman Catholic organizational structure. Juridically, St. Clement is not a legal entity, as are Protestant congregations, but is a part of the corporation known as the Catholic Archdiocese of Chicago. The extensive property of St. Clement is owned by that central corporation. If this local parish were to have any financial endowment, it would indeed have access to the proceeds from such capital, but the capital would be held by the Archdiocese of Chicago. Pastors and other clergy of the parish are appointed and transferred by the head of the Archdiocese of Chicago.

[23] Ibid., pp. 94–96.

When the parish was originally formed, Catholic lay persons requested that the bishop create a parish, leaving the decision as to who would be its pastor in the bishop's hands.

In matters of ritual, St. Clement uses the forms and contents prescribed for all Catholic churches of the archdiocese. At the present time, these forms are published in a "monthly missalet," which prescribes every detail of ritual activity except the content of the sermon.

About a thousand people attend Mass each Sunday at St. Clement. The seating capacity of the church is 700 persons—500 in the main church and 200 in the basement church. Worshipers have a choice of seven times at which to "fulfill their Sunday obligation." All these rituals follow the same form and structure, differing only in the content of the sermon. One ritual—"the folk Mass"—provides guitar accompaniment for the hymns sung at Mass, and these hymns are from contemporary writers of religious music.

In the late 1960s there seemed to be three distinct segments of the congregation of St. Clement. One segment was composed of older members of the congregation, persons who owned homes in the area and had been, or expected to be, part of St. Clement parish for many years. The second and largest segment was composed of the geographically mobile apartment dwellers. A local informant estimated that fewer than 10 percent of those married in St. Clement Church were living in the parish five years after their marriage. This extremely high rate of mobility prevents the formation of loyalties either to this unit of religious community or to the secular community of Lincoln Park. The third segment of the congregation was (and is) the members of the Young Adults' Club. This group maintains its contact with the parish through one of the younger assistant pastors and is most noteworthy for its practice of conducting experimental rituals outside the church premises. It is common for the pastor to learn of the activities of the Young Adults' Club only from rumor or from viewing the room in which an experimental ritual has been conducted after the ritual is over. The ritual activities of the Young Adults' Club are thus "underground": without the sanction or control of official authorities. The legitimacy of such experimentation is so delicate an issue in the Catholic concept of organizational procedures that its existence creates tensions between the pastor, who is more oriented to the traditions of the church as an organization, and those younger clergy who associate with the Young Adults' Club, who are more interested in responding to the felt needs of Catholics who wish to experiment with ritual form and content.

During the demonstrations of the summer of 1968, St. Clement turned down a request from other churches in the area to allow its buildings to be used as sleeping quarters for the demonstrators who had been forbidden the use of Lincoln Park by city officials.

Although church attendance in 1965 was perhaps 50 percent less than it had been in the late fifties, and although the pastor expressed concern about the parish's ability to maintain eight substantial buildings "with nothing much coming in," St. Clement is not yet a "dying church." Part of the reason is that it now serves an extremely cosmopolitan mixture of old German Catholics, young transients, Puerto Ricans, and blacks. The incoming population replacing the old German inhabitants of the parish is still Catholic enough and affluent enough to support basic parish activities. Further, the clergy and parishioners of St. Clement identify with the larger unit "the Catholic church" as much as, and in some cases more than, with St. Clement parish. Certainly some of the founding members of the parish think of it as peculiarly theirs. But many of these have moved out, and when they do, even though they are not discouraged from returning to St. Clement, they soon "become involved in their own local parish."

The transiency of St. Clement's congregation and the hierarchical structure of Roman Catholicism have combined to prevent the creation of a "liturgy team" in this congregation.[24] The parish has even found it difficult to maintain its own school board at full strength.

In the Church of the Three Crosses we see a change in the style of religious ritual beginning in 1965 with the congregation's quest for "involvement" and "commitment as coming from the people." In St. Paul we see that a new understanding of ritual begins with the revelation of hidden conflicts in the congregation on the occasion of the demonstrations at the Democratic Convention. In St. Clement the formation of new liturgical styles occurs in a semi-clandestine way in the Young Adults' Club. The reforms occurring in the main church maintain the traditional separations of clergy from laity and the separation of the content of ritual from the content of everyday life. There is, moreover, in St. Clement a degree of detachment of the churchgoers from the local center of ritual not found in Protestant churches in general. The centralized organizational structure of Catholicism and the transiency of the local congregation create a situation in which the participants in this Catholic ritual make almost

---

[24] A liturgy team is a committee of parishioners whose function is to construct those elements of the ritual not prescribed by central authority, or to choose elements of ritual from the repertoires provided by central authority.

no decision about the form or content of the worship service. The "consumption" of the ritual symbols has almost no corporate qualities, and is in this sense more privatized than Protestant worship. Those changes in religious ritual, therefore, which occur when a group of believers confronts a changing social milieu are almost entirely absent from the dynamics of worship at St. Clement. What goes on in the Young Adults' Club, we may assume, has elements of similarity to what goes on in the congregation of the Church of the Three Crosses and in the Worship and Sacrament Committee of St. Paul. One could try to verify the existence of such similarities between innovating Protestant congregations and "underground liturgies" in the Catholic church by using descriptions already published. But limitations of time and resources have prevented intensive field work on this phase of St. Clement's ritual.

This Catholic parish is distinctive in our group, however, because of the fact that the centralized organization of the Roman Catholic church has a tendency to push such local innovation into a semi-clandestine state and leave the publicly Catholic form of ritual in the hands of experts who do not have roots in the local milieu in which the product of their reforms is enacted.

ST. JAMES (MISSOURI SYNOD) LUTHERAN CHURCH

When in the 1840s the "Old St. Paul Church" split into two congregations, members of both persuasions were in the process of moving into North Town. The Missouri Synod congregation placed great emphasis on church-directed primary schools, and so this congregation's first presence in North Town was in the form of primary schools rather than houses of worship. Thus a primary school was founded in 1857 at the corner of Willow and Burling streets. For thirteen years, Missouri Synod Lutherans in North Town sent their children to a local church school and traveled down to Grand and LaSalle streets to worship in the original Missouri Synod St. Paul Church.

In 1869 the number of members of St. Paul in North Town warranted the founding of a new parish in that area. Therefore, St. James parish was founded, and the first church building was completed in 1870. Both the school and the church narrowly escaped the Great Fire of 1871. The prevailing wind confined the blaze to an area less than two blocks from these structures.

Between 1870 and 1905, St. James Church founded six more primary schools, which eventually became sites for other Missouri Synod Lutheran churches on Chicago's north side. By 1905 the church and educational activities of the St. James congregation were limited to the two buildings straddling the intersection of Dickens and Fremont streets in south-central Lincoln Park. In 1916 the old frame church building was torn down and replaced by the present brick structure on the same site.

At the turn of the century, St. James was serving Missouri Synod Lutherans over a wide area of Chicago's north side and counted approximately 2,000 "communicant members" in its congregation. In 1944 this membership was still slightly more than 1,000. By 1965, membership had decreased to approximately 500.

The organizational aspects of St. James have characteristics both of the congregational autonomy of St. Paul United Church of Christ and of the dependence on a central organization of St. Clement. This Lutheran congregation is a fiscal and corporate entity which calls and hires its pastor. The congregation is governed by the pastor-executive who works with a "voting membership" (approximately 15 percent of the male membership), which is the legislative body of the congregation, and a ten-man Board of Elders, which is the policy-making committee of the congregation. Pastors usually remain for life, and as a result St. James had only five pastors in the first hundred years of its history (1870–1970). The sixth pastor of St. James took office in 1971.

But St. James shares with other Missouri Synod churches strong affective ties with the larger organization. The Missouri Synod has been the most conservative mainline Protestant denomination in regard to the mergers of the "Ecumenical movement." It has its own seminaries, its own liberal arts colleges, and a system of primary and secondary schools. The teachers who serve in St. James parish school are recruited exclusively from Lutheran colleges.

Although Missouri Synod congregations have considerably more autonomy in composing their ritual than Roman Catholic parishes do, they still tend to depend on the forms created by synodal theologians and experts. The present form of worship used in St. James is that of *The Lutheran Hymnal,* most recently published in 1941 by the Concordia Press in St. Louis. Concordia Press has also published "ritual supplements" up to the present time, but none of these were in use in St. James in 1970.

With the calling of a new and younger pastor at the beginning of 1971, the members of St. James congregation saw the need for some reforms in their church organization and ritual. A layman (who is also principal of the church school) assisted the pastor in distributing communion. The congregation was considering allowing women to become voting members of the congregation. The church school has responded to the changing racial patterns of the area, and so about 50 percent of its students in 1970 were black and not members of St. James congregation.

But in 1971 the congregation still adhered to the set of separations and segmentations described above in connection with St. Paul Church. The pastor's role is highly differentiated in practice from that of the laity, even though the congregation firmly asserts its belief in "the priesthood of all believers." The congregation is one of the churches in Lincoln Park known for its nonparticipation in community affairs. One of its members is on the board of directors of the Lincoln Park Conservation Association, but in this position he does not represent his pastor or the congregation. When St. James was asked to provide sleeping space for out-of-town demonstrators in 1968, the pastor excused himself and the congregation on the grounds that the church was far from the scene of the demonstrations and that there were other, more "involved" churches nearer. He did not criticize the demonstrators—as at least one pastor in Lincoln Park did, by saying, "They have homes; they should go there and sleep in their parents' houses." He quietly abstained from getting involved.

The internal form and structure of ritual at St. James are part of the subject of the next chapter. From a social, secular, historical point of view, St. James is a middle-sized congregation of modest means, an unobtrusive and very conservative congregation in Lincoln Park. In 1971 this congregation was just beginning to think about revisions of its traditions.

SUMMARY

Although the four churches we are looking at are all "middle class" and white, they show wide variation on a number of important social and historical characteristics. It would undoubtedly be possible to sample a larger number of such churches, construct a correlation matrix based on these characteristics, and look for relationships between them and the kinds of ritual style we are going to describe in the following chapter. But this survey approach is not our central concern. Rather we want to center on the kinds of ritual change which might be used as dependent or independent variables in any such study, using this set of social, historical profiles as a preliminary but relatively rich examination of the context of those changes.

In the preceding descriptions, we have outlined several characteristics whose variance is important to consider when examining ritual change. These are (1) the denominational traditions of the churches as to their theology, their socioeconomic background, and their organizational structure; (2) the personality and belief systems of ministers and pastors; (3) the current socioeconomic status of the churches; (4) the occupational pattern of their members; (5) the place of the local congregation in the larger organizational structure of the denomination; and (6) the age structure of the congregation.

We have not included, up to this point, the geographic location of the church in the community area, because all four churches share the same ecological position—that is, all are in the same community area in which dramatic social and political changes and conflicts are occurring. In this respect, their common position is vastly different from that of outer-city or suburban churches and can be thought to have a distinctive effect on their religious practices. But it does not seem to matter whether a church is two hundred yards or eight blocks from the activity of the bulldozers. Even in those cases where changes in a congregation seem to be caused by proximity to a particular social movement—as, for example, the proximity of the Armitage Avenue Methodist Church to the center of the Young Lords' turf—there are churches much farther away which have become equally involved in such movements (in this case, the Parish of the Holy Covenant on the northern boundary of Lincoln Park), and churches just as close which have been less involved. (in this case, St. Teresa Roman Catholic Church and St. Vincent).[25]

The occurrence of "involvement" and certain kinds of change are related to the whole complex of variables just cited, and among these, in Lincoln Park, "ecological position" appears to be a constant rather than a variable. The order in which the six characteristics above are listed is an intuitive "rank order," and it would be valuable for survey research to try to verify such a ranking. But the image of the determination of behavior by such social characteristics is one which the ethnographer wishes to avoid. In pursuing our descriptions more concretely, we try to preserve the image of an individual con-

[25] Interaction ritual occurred in Armitage Avenue Church and in the Parish of the Holy Covenant, but I did not study either of them thoroughly.

gregation's freedom within constraints created by social and historical conditions.

Finally, in all the descriptions given up to this point, the one
factor which has not been clarified is the precise nature of changes in
ritual occurring in this kind of social setting. We now turn to such
changes.

CHAPTER 5

The Analysis of Ritual

In the next chapters, we shall examine in turn the settings, the internal structure, and the support institutions of the four rituals under consideration. But first let us consider the analytical framework which informs that examination.

SOCIAL CONTEXT

We are looking at the rituals of churches of the middle class in Lincoln Park because these churches stand "between" the churches of the powerful and the churches of the disinherited[1] and therefore face more continually the dilemma of being "culture religion" or "prophetic religion." A "church of the middle" is one which belongs to an established denomination, whose congregation has a durable and stable place in its local community, whose members are employed in middle-class occupations and therefore see themselves as full participants in the local and national social order.

WHOLE AND PARTS

There is a strong element of consistency in anthropologists' most general description of the function of religious ritual in social life: "Rituals function to encode messages about the nature of the world

---

[1] Milton Yinger reviews the literature on the churches of the disinherited (which he calls the churches of the disprivileged) in his *Sociology Looks at Religion* (New York: Collier-Macmillan, 1961), pp. 39–64.

and the actor's relationship to it; about definitions and interrelations."[2] Religious symbols are "the most general model which an individual or a group has of itself and its world. . . ."[3]

Religious symbol systems are products of men's meaning-giving activity; and, as products embedded in the arrangements of physical artifacts, regularized modes of motor activity, and specific forms of language, they have a facticity of their own and the status of relatively independent variable in the social milieu which is their context. Once produced out of the chaotic stuff of everyday life, they provide interpretive schemes[4] which then channel the social action of their adherents.

But this most general description of the function of ritual is not enough to clarify the impact of religion on a specific social-historical situation. We must raise the questions of *how* religious symbols perform this general function and what, if any, are the various structural elements of ritual which make it work.

We have already stated, for example, that the rituals of the churches in Lincoln Park remained "stable" between the time of the churches' founding in the late nineteenth century until the mid-1960s. Then, we said, some of the rituals "changed." In order to specify the nature of this stability and this change, we must look at rituals both as gestaltic wholes and as fabrications composed of interrelated parts.

That they are gestaltic wholes is indicated by comments of worshipers such as those I often heard after a Sunday morning service: "Well, I don't know about anyone else, but for me, *it happened* this morning." The cathartic, satisfying effect of the ritual is perceived as a single experience. In this respect, the parts of the ritual have a cumulative effect greater than—in fact, incommensurate with—the effects of the parts taken singly. But on the other hand, when we look at ritual in the process of transformation from one style to another, we see that this process is achieved in a piecemeal fashion: both by the rearrangement of the parts of the ritual and by the alteration of the properties of individual parts.

---

[2] M. G. Silverman, "Maximize Your Options: A Study in Values, Symbols, and Social Structure," in *Forms of Symbolic Action: Proceedings of the 1969 Annual Spring Meeting of the American Ethnological Society,* ed. Robert F. Spencer (Seattle: University of Washington Press, 1969), p. 109.

[3] Robert N. Bellah, "The Sociology of Religion," *International Encyclopedia of the Social Sciences,* vol. 13 (New York: Macmillan Co., 1968), p. 413.

[4] The phrase *interpretive scheme* is Thomas Luckmann's in *The Invisible Religion: The Transformation of Symbols in Industrial Society* (New York: Macmillan Co., 1967), p. 45 and *passim.*

Ritual is divided into portions analogous to the acts and scenes of a theatrical production. The longer of these divisions I have labeled *segments* of the ritual, and the several subdivisions of the segments we are examining are called *operations*. An operation is a unit of behavior, such as a song, a reading, an impromptu utterance, a sermon. Operations have a semi-autonomous existence and meaning. They may be moved from place to place in the ritual scenario, or dropped from or added to the ritual.

The number of segments in the four rituals varies from three to five. The number of operations ranges from fifteen to thirty. The larger variation in the number of operations is due to variations in the use of the communion service in the ritual. The portion of these rituals called eucharistic liturgy contains from eight to twelve operations proper to itself. The rest of the standard worship service contains fifteen to twenty operations. Since the Roman Catholic ritual always contains the eucharistic liturgy, it always has about thirty operations. When the Protestant rituals include the eucharistic liturgy, they too have close to thirty operations rather than fifteen.

The segments of these rituals are in some cases explicitly titled; operations are almost always titled. These titles of segments are exegetical in character. That is, they raise to explicit consciousness the theological structure of a given ritual, explaining the relationship of instrumental symbols to dominant symbols. As an example, here is one of the bulletins given to worshipers on Sunday morning at The Church of the Three Crosses (September 27, 1970):

PREPARATION FOR THE WORD
    The Prelude
    The Call to Awareness
    The Hymn, No. 10
    The Confession
    The Assurance
    The Song
THE CONFRONTATION WITH THE WORD
    The Word from Scripture
    The Secular Reading
    The Shared Word
    The Silent Reflection
THE RESPONSE TO THE WORD
    The Congregational Concerns
    The Lord's Prayer
    The Offering

> The Offertory
> The Doxology
> The Unison Reminder
> The Hymn
> The Dreams for Celebration
> The Unison Chorus Amen
> The Postlude

Explicit titles seem to occur in situations of ritual change, where the theological import of the ritual is problematic. Where the operations of the ritual are not grouped into titled units, this segmentation is indicated in other ways. We find directions in the weekly bulletin that "latecomers may be seated at this time"—that is, at the time between segments of the ritual performance. Untitled segments indicate that the theological structure of the ritual is not considered problematic and can therefore be taken for granted.

Before 1965, the changes in the rituals under study here were limited to the content of operations. It is only since the mid-sixties that changes in the labels of segments, the number of segments, and the order, behavioral style, and number of operations began to occur.

THREE LEVELS OF MEANING

In chapter 1, I referred to Victor Turner's distinction among three levels of meaning in symbols and the rituals in which they are set. These levels or "fields" of meaning vary, according to Turner, in their degree of consciousness. Level 1, the exegetical meaning, is the most fully conscious, and level 3, the positional meaning, is the most unconscious.[5] The assumption of this analytical scheme is, of course, that different observable aspects of ritual reliably express different psychic levels of meaning.[6]

The kinds of data which contain these levels of meaning are as follows: (1) The exegetical meaning is found in the interpretations of ritual made by those who participate in it, and in the content of

---

[5] In Turner's words, the exegetical, operational, and positional meanings contain, respectively, the conscious meaning and some of the latent sense, the latent sense and some of the hidden sense, and the hidden sense of the symbolic expression. See Victor W. Turner, *The Drums of Affliction* (Oxford: Clarendon Press, 1968), p. 83.

[6] The stability of ritual patterns and of linguistic usage in Africa apparently eliminated the possibility of this kind of expression of latent-hidden meanings.

the verbal utterances of the ritual itself.[7] (2) The operational meaning is contained in the motor activity performed in the course of ritual (for example, processions, bowing, sitting, handling of objects) and in that aspect of language known as "style" (especially the difference between archaic and contemporary linguistic forms). (3) The positional meaning of ritual is contained in the arrangements of the space used in the performance of ritual. These spatial arrangements are for the most part symbolic rather than technical-practical. The fact that their meaning remains "hidden" means that it is the least accessible to the normal (that is, "conscious") range of attention of the participants.

In accepting the assumption that ritual has latent and hidden meanings as well as conscious ones, we open the door to an exceedingly wide range of interpretations. Among such interpretations are the psychoanalytic, the "social field" perspectives of Victor Turner, the psychic-development perspective of Philip Slater, and the cultural-evolution perspective of Robert Bellah.

Bettelheim's *Symbolic Wounds*[8] is an example of the psychoanalytic interpretation of ritual. Two general characteristics of such interpretations are that they regard most indigenous interpretations of ritual as analogous to the rationalizations by which neurotics explain and justify their behavior, and that they "claim to recognize in the structure and action context of ritual symbols material derived from what they consider to be the universal experiences of human infancy in the family situation."[9] Thus the psychoanalytic interpretation tends to show how all religious rituals and symbols are identical, to continually rediscover the common conditions of the human organism in the family and society. Although such interpretations are frequently valid as far as they go, they do little to reveal the variance in the use of religious symbols which also has the power to shed light on the meaning of this phenomenon.

Victor Turner of course accepts the general validity of psychoanalytic interpretations, but he points out that even unconscious mean-

[7] In studying African rituals, Turner had to rely on the interpretations of informants. In studying American Christian rituals, we find that the ritual itself is often a conscious definition of its own meaning, as for example when the titles of the segments of a ritual are "Preparation for the Word, Encounter with the Word, Response to the Word."

[8] Bruno Bettelheim, *Symbolic Wounds: Puberty Rites and the Envious Male* (Glencoe, Ill.: Free Press, 1964).

[9] Victor W. Turner, *The Forest of Symbols: Aspects of Ndembu Ritual* (Ithaca, N.Y.: Cornell University Press, 1967), p. 34.

ings often refer to specific patterns of social and political interaction
within the groups performing the ritual:

> The psychoanalyst . . . must . . . attach greater significance than he now
> does to social factors in the analysis of ritual symbolism. . . . "One must
> learn to go underneath the symbol to the reality which it represents and
> which gives it its meaning. No religions are false, all answer, though in dif-
> ferent ways, to the given conditions of human existence." (Durkheim, *Ele-
> mentary Forms of Religious Life*, pp. 2–3.) Among those given conditions,
> the arrangement of society into structured groupings, discrepancies be-
> tween the principles that organize those groupings, economic collaboration
> and competition, schism within groups and opposition between groups—
> in short, all those things with which the social aspect of ritual symbolism is
> concerned—are surely of at least equal importance with biophysical drives
> and early conditioning in the elementary family.[10]

Turner further observes that the difference between "ritual symbols" on the one hand and "psychic symbols" on the other is that
the former are "gross means of handling *social* and *natural* reality"
while the latter are "dominantly fashioned under the influence of
inner drives."[11] Therefore, when we examine the symbols that occur
in the context of ritual—when we go to church on Sunday, for instance—we may expect to find latent and hidden meanings which
refer to the dominant power fields of the cultural and social milieu
of the ritual, whether those power fields are concerned with the occurence of disease and the tensions of a matrilineal-virilocal kinship
system, as in the Ndembu, or with building codes, bulldozers, and
the demonstrations of yippies in Lincoln Park.

One way of expressing Turner's anthropological perspective on
ritual is to say that the person who performs ritual is aware of the
power fields defined by social boundaries and expressed in social
interactions but cannot articulate them verbally. Since these social
and political boundaries and interactions are part of the integral field
of striving for identity, meaning, and personal achievement, religious
ritual refers to them and includes them in an integral system of
meaning whose summary form is the set of "common goals and
values" which most broadly characterize any given society.

This way of expressing Turner's perspective simply highlights the
fact that an ego-and-environment field is an important image and
paradigm for analyzing religious ritual. Anthropologists have been
most acute in demonstrating the connection between the contemporary social, cultural, and political environment and the motor

[10] Ibid., p. 37.
[11] Ibid.

activity, spatial arrangements, and symbols of religious ritual.[12] But they have also accepted—because the data from primitive religions warrant it—a stable valence relationship between ego and the environment which includes and circumscribes it. That is, the degree of the autonomy of ego vis-à-vis the forces which impinge on it from its environment—forces which take the form of disease-bringing spirits, life-giving fauna and flora, generational, sexual, and kin-based elements of social structure—tends to remain stable in all the rituals studied by anthropologists concerned with tribal Africa.

When we turn, however, to ego-psychologists who are concerned with the cultural expressions of the development of ego autonomy, we find analyses of group processes such as ritual in which *differences* in the degree of ego autonomy vis-à-vis environment are the central issue. In studies such as Philip Slater's *Microcosm*[13] the issue for analysis is not so much the intermingling of religious-symbolic and social environments as the variance in the degree of autonomy of ego with respect to all such environments.

From the developmental perspective of the ego-psychologist, the way a group handles symbols shows an evolutionary process. Slater speaks of "emergent groups" which use symbols and rituals to aid their collective efforts to define the boundaries of the egos of the members of the groups. Different religious rituals manifest different degrees of awareness of the separation of individuals from the social mass, and these different degrees of awareness of autonomy are the basis for speaking of the "evolution of religion." There is a "continuum of boundary awareness"[14] expressed by rituals, and the boundary in question is between ego and environment: environment being both the other persons within the group performing the ritual and the material, social, and political world outside the group.

The evolution of personal autonomy is the underlying paradigm for Robert N. Bellah's discussion of the evolution of religion.[15] Slater says of Bellah's discussion:

[12] There are many other contributions to this discussion besides the work of Turner. One of the most interesting for the analysis expressed in this book is Mary Douglas, *Purity and Danger: An Analysis of Concepts of Pollution and Taboo* (London: Routledge and Kegan Paul, 1966). Douglas demonstrates that parts of the human body easily come to stand for parts of society, and that therefore bodily postures and motor activities frequently refer to culturally defined social attitudes and social and political trends and processes.

[13] Philip E. Slater, *Microcosm: Structural, Psychological and Religious Evolution in Groups* (New York: John Wiley, 1966).

[14] Ibid., p. 228.

[15] Robert N. Bellah, "Religious Evolution," *American Sociological Review* 29 (June 1964): 358–74.

Bellah's stages, while representing complex empirical amalgams rather than deductively derived segments of a single strand, still reveal a clear relationship with the continuum of boundary awareness and its associated mechanisms. Thus Bellah's first phase, "primitive religion" is characterized by weak and elastic distinctions between self and world, between mythical and empirical worlds, and between religious and other roles. "Archaic religion" contains more characterization of mythical beings . . . , an elaborated cosmology, priestly roles and a sharper distinction between "men as subjects and gods as objects," with the consequent emergence of communications systems such as worship and sacrifice and of "a new degree of freedom as well, perhaps, as an increased burden of anxiety." "Historical religion" introduces a sharp dualism between the empirical cosmos . . . and life-after-death. "Early modern religion" is essentially equated with the Protestant reformation and evinces a return to worldly involvement, a collapsing of both symbolic and organizational hierarchies. . . . Bellah is a little vague about "modern religion," but stresses its abandonment of dualism for an "infinitely multiplex" structure, the further detachment from religious specialists, the intensification of awareness of personal responsibility for religious symbolization, and the fact that "culture and personality have come to be viewed as endlessly revisable."[16]

The works of Bettelheim, Turner, Slater, and Bellah show that there are a number of different and valid ways of interpreting ritual. Given the nature of the data of this study, we shall have to be selective in the interpretations we try to give. We will leave aside the fruitful insights of the "pure" psychoanalysts such as Bettelheim, because such interpretations are not the province of the social anthropologist. We will accept as a guiding principle of investigation the methodological advice of Victor Turner that the manifestations of latent and hidden meanings of ritual can reliably be found in certain kinds of data. These kinds of data are the patterns of motor activity performed in ritual and the spatial arrangements constructed for it. What people do in church and how they arrange the space for their worship, therefore, are just as meaningful as what they say the ritual means to them.

What we take from Philip Slater is simply his general perspective that the latent and hidden meanings of ritual will reveal differences in the degree of autonomy and the kinds of autonomy that characterize the relationship between the ego of the individual worshipers and their ritual environment. Not only can believers use religious symbols and rituals to define their social world; they can use them more or less consciously, more or less "autonomously." In particular, they can depend on others—institutional authorities—to make their

---

[16] Slater, p. 228.

symbols for them, or they can take to themselves the task of making their own symbols and rituals.

From Bellah we draw another aspect of our general perspective. That is that over time, long periods of time, historically new forms of religion occur. Furthermore, the novelty of these new forms of religion lies in the manner in which they portray the relation between the sacred and the profane. From Bellah we draw the awareness that ritual styles express the "given conditions of human existence"; that is, they not only are responses to personal styles of relationship of individual to group—as Slater sees—but also are created by large-scale social and cultural trends. Following Bellah, we try to portray the wider social situation of local rituals in as much detail as possible.

CHAPTER 6

Comparative Patterns
in Lincoln Park
1: The Settings of Ritual

We now turn to a comparison of the rituals of the four churches studied. We will focus on the similarities and differences which are both structural and customary. These are differences in the basic patterns of the rituals which reveal participants' different understandings of the relationship between the individual worshipers and the symbols they handle in ritual.

We divide the setting of ritual into two parts: the temporal setting and the spatial setting. The temporal setting is simply the time chosen for worship. The spatial setting is the nature of the place—in this case, the building—chosen to perform ritual. This includes the decorations of the building and its separateness from the space surrounding it.

The spatial and temporal settings of the four rituals are summarized in table 5. Clearly, these four churches differ in the permeability of the spatial boundaries they erect between the sacred and profane aspects of the world. In choosing a time for ritual, they also differ in the absoluteness of the authority of the traditions specifying the proper time for ritual.

TEMPORAL SETTING

Common to all four rituals is the choice of Sunday as the day of worship. This choice is of course due to the Christian interpretation of

TABLE 5.   Spatial and Temporal Settings of the Four Rituals

	Three Crosses	St. Paul	St. Clement	St. James
Sunday is usual day for worship	+	+	+	+
The building is marked as religious	+	+	+	+
A room used exclusively for worship	−	+	+	+
Secular use of church building	+	+	−	−
Ritual performed in unmarked sites outside the building	+	−	−	−

the seven days of Creation narrated in the Book of Genesis in the Bible. This interpretation is strengthened by the traditional belief that Jesus rose from the grave on a Sunday. This is the exegetical meaning of Sunday. It is chosen as the day for worship because it is the day on which God rested after creating the world and the day on which Jesus rose from the dead.

There is also an operational meaning of Sunday as the day for worship, and this meaning is different in mid-twentieth-century America than it was in Europe in the Middle Ages. Going to church on Sunday is no longer a universal custom of society. Participation in ritual begins, as one informant notes, on Saturday night, "when you have to make decisions about how late you are going to stay out and when you are going to prepare your meals for Sunday." Going to church on Sunday often forces the participants in ritual to deviate from more common use of the hours of that day. When, in the ritual, the participants refer to themselves as "a people set apart," they not only are repeating the words of the ancient Israelites but are using an image substantiated in part by their experience of being different from their co-workers and neighbors in their use of Sunday morning.

The positional meaning of the day of worship—occurring as it does at regular seven-day intervals throughout the year—is that Sunday rituals are meant to interpret "everyday life" rather than to commemorate moments of passage from one social condition to another. There are, in all these churches, specialized rituals for important transitional situations of the life cycle, such as those of funerals, marriages, ordination to the ministry, confirmation, and baptism. Sunday worship, by contrast, expresses a continuous encounter with the sacred and in this respect differs from rites of passage in everyday life, which are occasional, marking major changes in the relationship of individuals to the social group.[1]

The choice of the hour on Sunday at which worship is performed has become more of a technical-practical ("logistical," as one pastor said) matter. But there is also evidence that the hour of eleven o'clock was symbolic as well as practical.

> I'm not sure, now, timewise, to how much that comes; that comes; that was probably a year after we came. But that was a crucial decision . . . to change the worship hour from eleven o'clock, which it had always been, to ten o'clock. This would do two things: it would allow, first of all, for a talkback we initiated, so the people could talk back to the sermon. There could be more give and take following up what was happening in the service. And second of all, [it would allow] the Spanish congregation—which had been down in the basement, so to speak, with a little stage, and in an area where the traffic noises were there, and people would come, always interrupting part of their service—. . . to worship in the sanctuary. And well, it was a big hassle. It was a lot of hassle, about giving up the eleven o'clock hour. The eleven o'clock hour is the Protestant hour for worship. And it's a sacred hour. I mean, I don't know why. . . . But it finally got battled through, and we were able to switch around so that the talkback became an integral part of the service.

The eleven o'clock hour did originally have a practical cause: "It emerged as the most convenient hour between the two daily milkings in an agrarian culture."[2] But the pastor's comment, "I don't know why . . . ," indicates that the practical reason had been forgotten, and for some believers eleven o'clock had become a sacred hour.

Those persons who have this attitude toward the details of the ritual "cannot distinguish between form and content," says one pastor. Criticism of new rituals by such persons generally focuses on small details such as the introduction of banners for decorating the room for worship. For them, the whole ritual is handed down, and any change is an arrogation to self of the authority of tradition. Thus, the struggle to change the hour of worship which occurred in the Church of the Three Crosses was a struggle about the authority of tradition versus the authority of the members of the congregation themselves.

[1] Examples of rituals from other times and traditions which express this continuing relationship between the sacred and the profane are numerous. The Islamic custom of praying five times every twenty-four hours and the "canonical hours" of the Christian monastic communities are two such examples. The Sunday worship service gathers the believing community together with the same regularity as these other rituals, although not with the same frequency.

[2] William A. Holmes, *Tomorrow's Church: A Cosmopolitan Community* (New York: Abingdon Press, 1968), p. 80.

SPATIAL SETTING

In 1965, all of the rituals we are studying were performed in a space specifically set aside for the performance of ritual. This space was distinguished from buildings designated for profane usage by a style of architecture. Between 1965 and 1970, some rituals tended to move out of a space set apart. One example of this trend was the underground Catholics' practice of celebrating Mass in the home. Another manifestation of this trend was the practice of some churches of permitting the place of worship to be used for secular activities such as community meetings.

All the church buildings we are considering were originally of the genre of space which Mircea Eliade calls "temples": physical structures which define the boundaries between sacred and profane space. We cannot apply all the details of Eliade's phenomenology of temples to the churches in Lincoln Park. But we can call attention to changes in the *permeability* of the boundaries between the sacred and the profane that have occurred in these churches. These changes imply changes in the intensity of the sacredness of the sacred space which the boundaries enclose. Such changes are changes in the operational and positional meaning of the physical setting of ritual.

The performance of religious ritual in American society is commonly referred to as "going to church." This journey to the church is part of the symbolic structure of the ritual; therefore, the physical appearance of the building expresses some aspects of the center of society and of moral values as perceived by the believers. The churches in Lincoln Park display an interesting variety in physical appearance.

The Church of the Three Crosses is a white frame building, referred to by its congregation as "the little country church in the city." This reference is made with good-natured wryness or some other indication that the congregation has not chosen to cling to the rural heritage of its church. A further indication of lack of commitment to a rural way of life is seen in the plans the congregation made for a new church building, to be erected on land obtained in the process of urban renewal. The new church was to be a "community center," built of brick and reinforced concrete, including a sculptured monument to the destruction of the old city wrought by urban renewal, a monument built of rubble from old buildings. The plan of the new building, moreover, called for the construction, not of a room permanently set aside for worship by this single congregation, but of an "ecumenical center" which would be available to the secular-profane community, for cultural and political meetings as well as various religious meetings.

During the period from 1965 to 1970, moreover, the relation of the present church building to the "rest of the world" changed. The permeability of the boundary between the world represented by the building and the profane world decreased. This was indicated most clearly by the manner in which the building was opened to the use of the "community." The building has two floors. The ground floor contains a large meeting hall, a small kitchen, and three smaller rooms suitable for offices or classrooms. These rooms had always been used for secular (though usually church-related) activities. During the period mentioned, however, the second floor of the building, containing the room set aside for worship, was also opened for secular use. Since the needs of various groups in the community for meeting space were occasionally more than could be accommodated by the first floor, the "sanctuary" was also made available. The decision to do this was the result of discussion and conscious decision by the congregation. Their sacred space, it was decided, was not so sacred that it could not be used for secular activities.

During this time also, this congregation began the practice of holding worship outdoors. On certain occasions in the spring and summer, when the weather was beautiful, they met at the church building and then walked in informal groups to nearby Lincoln Park, sat down on the grass and held their usual worship service, and took part in a group picnic meal afterward.

The second church in our study—St. Paul—is a monument to the prestige and German cultural heritage of the congregation. The new church is less ornate than the old one, which burned down in 1955, but it was built at the direction of older members of the congregation and with financial help from wealthy families which had been associated with the old church for more than a generation. In this complex of buildings, the church proper—referred to as the "sanctuary"—is only one room out of many. Although many parts of these buildings are used for secular purposes (day-care center, primary-school activities, club meetings, community meetings), the sanctuary is used only for worship. Its boundaries are impermeable to profane usage. These rooms give physical form to a cosmology in which there is a distinctively "sacred" zone of the "really real," separated from the "rest of the world." When worshipers journey to this room, the operational meaning of their journey is to move from one world into another.

When the "experimental" worship was begun in this church (in 1970), it was first held in a classroom. At this time, banners made of felt were hung in the room for the time of worship, to temporarily mark the space as sacred. The subject of these decorations was raised at the meetings of the worship task force, and it was agreed that such markings were necessary to create a suitable site for ritual. After two rituals in such secular settings, the experimental service was moved to a chapel on the church premises. This small church, built by a wealthy benefactor of the congregation, had customarily been used for weddings and for the communion service of the congregation, held four or five times a year.

This experimental ritual lasted only six months. It attracted thirty-five persons the first two weeks, but attendance rapidly dropped. The final worship service in this phase of the congregation's experiment was attended by two ministers, the wife of one of the ministers, one other member of the congregation, and the author of this study. This drop in attendance seemed to be related to the innovators' inability to clarify for themselves the proper degree of permeability of the boundary between the sacred and the profane.[3] During the summer, they did meet in the evening, on the church lawn, but were not satisfied with the results of this experiment.

The third church, St. Clement, is a Roman Catholic church built in Byzantine style. The Roman Catholic cathedral in St. Louis, Missouri, was used as a model[4] because of its meaning for the first pastor of the parish. The resemblance to the St. Louis cathedral and the Italian marble and artwork in the church symbolize relationships to the long and durable past of the Roman Catholic church, which includes memories of Byzantine glory.

The operational meaning of the journey to this building on Sunday morning is acceptance of that past glory as a center of the contemporary cosmos.

The physical plant of the parish includes two rooms set aside for ritual. Below the main church there is a basement church, in which the "folk mass" is celebrated. Neither of these rooms is used for any purpose other than ritual. Experiments with new forms of ritual (the underground liturgy) take place in parishioners' homes or in secular meeting rooms on church premises. This use of secular prem-

---

[3] For a detailed discussion of what actually happened to this experimental ritual, see chapter 9.

[4] The architects for the St. Louis cathedral drew the plans for this smaller replica of that building.

ises for sacred ritual is partly due to the disapproval by church authorities of such experimentation, but it is also due to the unsuitability of the sacred premises themselves. They are enclosed in imposing walls and doorways and furnished with pews, statues, paintings, stained-glass windows, and lighting and acoustical effects which create an unmistakable and *exclusively* other-worldly atmosphere. The "rest of the world" is indeed far away in this setting.

The fourth church—St. James—does not express a particular cultural orientation in the manner of the others. Its physical appearance does not recall the rural past, the affluence of a localized ethnic settlement, or Byzantine glory. This church is distinctive for its modesty and ordinary quality. It is a red brick structure which, but for the steeple, stained-glass windows, and cruciform floor plan, might be a large apartment building. This is in keeping with the life style of the German working-class congregation. The church plant includes three buildings: the primary school and the church, kitty-corner from one another, and the pastor's residence next door to the church. The school and the basement of the church are used for secular activities, all of which are church-related. Because the buildings are located in a quiet neighborhood (not near the park or directly in the way of new social movements) and are not of imposing size, and because members of the congregation have not been in leadership roles in the community, there has never been much demand that the physical plant be used to meet needs other than those of the congregation. Parish clubs, teenagers of the families of the congregation, and parents of the schoolchildren use the premises for their meetings.

The sanctuary of the church, however, is used exclusively for worship. Because the social distance of the congregation from the nonworshiping local community is already great, the difference between the sacred premises and the secular premises of the church buildings is not indicated sharply by differences in the frequency of use. In a quiet setting, the sanctuary is simply more quiet. In the period between 1965 and 1970, the patterns of use of these buildings was very stable.

SUMMARY

The common temporal settings of the four rituals we are studying simply shows that they all are indebted to the same mainstream of

Christian tradition. Where the hour on Sunday had become a part
of a church's tradition, the struggle to change that hour shows the
force of tradition and the manner in which it is opposed. When not
changed by authoritative command, the task of changing tradition
generates much anxiety, which is expressed in emotionally charged
discussions.

The spatial settings we discussed have a wide range of exegetical
meanings. The church buildings stand for many different confes-
sional (denominational) and local traditions, for many different relationships to the subcultural past, as befits the ethnic mosaic of the
Lincoln Park area. Operationally and positionally, however, the
spatial settings show a more unidimensional variation, that of the
permeability of the boundary between the sacred world and the
profane world. Three of these church buildings—St. Paul, St. Clement,
and St. James—symbolize a dualism which sharply distinguishes the
sacred from the profane. Protestant churches as well as Catholic
churches portray this dualism. The Church of the Three Crosses
clearly symbolizes a move from such a dualism to symbolizing the
"multiplex" world of "modern" religion.[5] The movement of ritual
from church buildings into homes, secular meeting rooms, and public
parks also shows the breakdown of a dualistic cosmology.

[5] Robert N. Bellah, "Religious Evolution," *American Sociological Review* 29
(June 1964): pp. 358–74. Although the official theology of Protestant churches
still retains the elements of what Bellah calls "early modern religion"—such as a
new involvement in the world and the collapse of symbolic and organizational
hierarchies—the *practice* of the churches in Lincoln Park shows that they have
reverted to the cosmology of historic religions. Although Protestants assert the
principle of the priesthood of all believers, this principle is not realized in practice. As we shall see, there is clear differentiation between clerical and lay roles
in ritual, and this difference is now justified by reference to secular models—
such as the need for *expertise*—rather than the idiom of theological hierarchies.
Perhaps this reversal of the evolutionary order is the result of the "mortgages
to the past" to which Bellah refers. It is also interesting that Luther himself re-
coiled from the autonomy of his early years as a reformer and sided with secular
authorities in putting down the Peasants' Revolt. (See Erik Erikson, *Young Man
Luther* [New York: Norton, 1958].)

CHAPTER 7

Comparative Patterns in Lincoln Park
2: The Internal Structure in Ritual

The patterned differences in the settings of our four rituals occur also in their internal structures. That is, the manner in which these rituals are actually performed on Sunday morning exhibits patterns that justify classifying them as examples of mass ritual on the one hand and interaction ritual on the other. These differences are *structural* in nature, in the sense that the term is used here, meaning that the differences occur systematically at all three levels of meaning: exegetical, operational, positional.

When we classify these rituals by their structural differences, we treat them differently from the conventional classification system, which starts by distinguishing among rituals (and churches) according to whether they are Protestant, Roman Catholic, or Jewish. This classification technique can extend to other "religions" such as Buddhism, Hinduism, occultism, and so on. Such classifications are important, but the structural classification which distinguishes between mass ritual and interaction ritual cuts across these lines of affiliation. These structural differences may exist with in *any* religious tradition, we imply. Our further claim is that these structural differences are "real." Therefore, when they exist within a religious group with common historical background, they indicate substantially different religious world views within that group. In this view, therefore, "Catholic"

99

or "Methodist" or any other such classification does not unequivo-
cally stand for "the same religion." Within such groups there may be
different and conflicting operative cosmologies. The manifestation of
such differences is the occurrence of mass ritual on the one hand and
interaction ritual on the other.

The conventional classification system is, however, based on an
aspect of structure. This aspect is "esoteric exegesis"; for the exegetical meaning of a ritual has two parts, one esoteric and one exoteric.
The esoteric exegesis is the meaning attributed to ritual by experts
and specialists. The exoteric exegesis is the interpretation of lay participants.[1] In regard to the rituals of this study, the esoteric exegesis
is a *theology*. One way of describing theologies is that they are what
clergy learn in seminaries and divinity schools. As such, theologies
derive their vocabulary from historical traditions. Therefore, when I
talked to the clergy in Lincoln Park, I found that on the basis of
their official theological interpretation of ritual, the two kinds of
ritual I encountered were Protestant and Roman Catholic. Whatever
"theology" of mass ritual versus interaction ritual may presently
exist is still emerging. It therefore exists, not at the level of official
documents and training programs, but at the level of informal and
lay interpretations.[2]

Table 6 summarizes the structural differences among the four
rituals.

EXOTERIC INTERPRETATIONS

Some Catholics and some Protestants in Lincoln Park express an "objective" interpretation of ritual, and some of each group express an
"egoic" interpretation.[3]

[1] Clergymen often express both esoteric and exoteric interpretations of ritual.
This is due to the fact that they express their seminary training, on the one
hand, and their contact with their congregation, on the other. The cues to when
they are giving exegesis are such phrases as "what it means in the strict sense,"
"what theology says," and so forth, as contrasted to phrases such as "what it
means to the people," "what we are trying to do here," and so forth.

[2] Some expressions of the Protestant-Catholic distinction are that Protestant
ministers cite Protestant theologians, and Catholic priests cite "the teachings of
the church" and Catholic theologians. Also, Catholic priests refer to their ritual
(the Mass) as a "sacrament," and emphasize the importance of communion.
Protestant pastors regard Roman Catholic "sacramentalism" as suspect, and emphasize the "hearing of the word" in describing their liturgy.

[3] There is apparently a great variety of styles in underground Roman Catholic
rituals. Some of them show a clear trend toward independence from tradition

TABLE 6. Structural Differences Among the Four Rituals

Element of Internal Structure	Three Crosses	St. Paul	St. Clement	St. James
(Exegetical)				
Official theology	Protestant	Protestant	Catholic	Protestant
Local exegesis	Egoic	Objective	Objective	Objective
(Operational)				
Distinctive clothing for clergy	No	Yes	Yes	Yes
Processions	No rank order of participants	Hierarchical	Hierarchical	Hierarchical
Lay initiation of sacred action	Usual	Rare	No	No
Tradition-prescribed order of ritual	No	Yes	Yes	Yes
Linguistic style	Includes slang	Archaic	Modern	Archaic
Usual musical instrument	Organ and guitar	Organ	Organ	Organ
Secular reading	Usual	Never	Never	Never
Talkback	Customary	No	No	No
(Positional)				
Raised stage for center of ritual	No	Yes	Yes	Yes
Railing between "central" and "lay" spaces	No	Yes	Yes	Yes

An "objective" interpretation of the Sunday morning service portrays it as a mode of communication between a pre-existing, structured sacred cosmos whose content and structure are independent of the conscious, voluntary activities of the worshiper's ego. For example:

> I am among those who would agree in some ways with Karl Barth, and his understanding that God has revealed himself in events which man has very little to do with. I'm not so sure that the idea that we all have equal access to God takes seriously the revelation of God in Jesus Christ.

Another form of objective interpretation of ritual is the statement often made by "conservative" members of churches in Lincoln Park: "I like the formal prayers." By "formal" prayers they mean those which are printed in a program or recited from memory, and which are traditional. They are prayers which are not ex tempore or impromptu but emanate from some authoritative source. The authority of the source seems to be proportional to its distance from the ego of the worshiper. That is, the least authoritative would be a prayer composed by the worshiper himself; then, one composed by a group of church members; then, one composed by the pastor; then, one in traditional use and printed in a hymnal or prayer book; then, one from the Bible.

The objective interpretation of ritual frequently mentions the importance of the experience of awe:

> It does give me a feeling of awe. I don't know why I'm awed by a sense of order and a certain kind of dignity, maybe even beauty, either through music or through the colors and arrangement of architecture. . . . I don't know why I'm *not* awed when you bring something off in community.

Rudolph Otto in *The Idea of the Holy* has commented on awe as an encounter with the "wholly Other." The "order" and "dignity" of the source of awe betoken the objectivity and the distance from self of the wholly Other. It is reality *set apart,* impinging from outside on the person who worships. That is, it impinges on the boundaries of one's self. It is not "from me" but from "elsewhere."

One psychological interpretation of this "orderly awful" is that it

---

and hierarchical authority and a high degree of interaction among participants, as well as interaction between participants and symbolic elements of ritual. Some underground rituals which I have observed, however, show much ambivalence concerning the proper degree of autonomy to be expressed with regard to traditional forms. My observation of such rituals has not been systematic and so does not form part of the data for this study. It would take systematic study to determine whether underground Catholics oppose only certain policies of sacred hierarchs, or whether they oppose such hierarchy in principle.

is a domesticated unconscious. The "oceanic experience"—which is a sudden awareness of the indefinitely extended range of unconscious knowledge and desires—is partially dangerous, and so is channeled and rendered orderly by tradition.[4] Certain modes of music, architecture, and style of sermons and prayers, the unhurried and predictable movements of the ritual, protect the participant from being engulfed in the total novelty of alternate meanings arising from the unconscious.[5]

The interpretation which values these ritual behaviors also protects the symbol system in question from revision. It is not the case that such a symbol system is *never* revised, but only that it is not revised during this kind of ritual. Revisions which do occur tend to occur hierarchically and from the center. That is, experts and specialists raise among themselves the issues for revision, work out the changes,

anomy

[4] The oceanic experience is closely linked to the phenomenon of anomie. If we admit of degrees of oceanic experience, we may say that the two are one and the same phenomenon. The two labels for this phenomenon occur because it can be defined by either its social referent or its psychic referent. The social referent of the phenomenon is that norms no longer impinge on a person. The anomic experience is not knowing what to *do*. The psychic referent is that this "not knowing what to do" is also a flooding of the mind with all sorts of suggestions: fantasies, theories, questions. All these possibilities confuse. The confusion of myriad possibilities is precisely the other side of the coin of the absence of social norms.

[5] This "psychological" interpretation is also sociological if "the unconscious" is a source of symbol systems. We know that symbol systems are social and cultural artifacts once they are produced, and that as such they affect empirical human behavior. But the present discussion touches on the issue of where symbol systems come from. What is their source and how are they made? The objective interpretation of ritual takes a stand on these issues. Its stand is that ritual—with respect to the individual worshiper—does not come "from me." It says that ritual and its attendant symbol system come from tradition and hierarchical authorities: sources which are "outside of" and "set apart from" me. The egoic interpretation of ritual—as we shall see immediately—says otherwise. It says ritual does come "from me." If the "me" in each instance were to be the unconscious of the speaker in question, that would fit. Thus, we must mention this issue of the unconscious even now. But since we are engaged in a cumulative argument, we must see all the empirical data before we have the whole argument in hand.

We can, however, clarify some terms. C. G. Jung speaks of the ego and the self. The *ego* is the seat of conscious activity. For any individual, ego is the referent of any "I" statement (I did that, I believe this, etc.). *Self* is a whole which includes this seat of conscious activity plus all unconscious knowledge, desires, and so on. That there is more to an individual's knowledge and desire than is encompassed by the ego is manifested in arguments of the pattern in which A says, "I didn't mean it," and B says, "You did too." The fact that B may be right shows that there is more to A than A is aware of. This "more" is, in one idiom, unconscious. In Jung's idiom, this "more" is part of self but not part of ego.

and hand them down to lay people. Such specialists may (or may not) be finely attuned to the "needs of the people" or "contemporary events." But the point is that it is the specialists and not the "people" who actually formulate the changes in the symbol system.

In this manner, the objective interpretation of ritual harmonizes well with rather calcified roles in the conduct of worship. The objectivity of the interpretation along with the rigidity of roles in ritual serves to keep a particular symbol system intact. An "intact" symbol system, in this context, is a world view, a *meaning* system. It is a set of symbols which clearly and consistently relates technical facts to a moral order. The foundations of good and evil are known and articulated in discrete symbols, concepts, and propositions. Action in the world, therefore, can be judged by reference to these symbols, concepts, and propositions. In this manner a symbol system couched in an objective interpretation of ritual preserves the order of the world. In providing this stable context for right action, it fulfills a fundamental social function: it enables actors to distinguish between good and evil.

An "egoic" interpretation of the Sunday morning ritual portrays it as a codification of the emergent intentions, wishes, and beliefs of the persons who participate in the ritual:

> I see the service as, let's say, the presentation of the word, the confrontation, the response to the word. The word that is shared is from Scripture, and sometimes from the secular word, or a shared word is sometimes from the sermon, from a person, or then another person, from somewhere in the congregation. I think that the greatness of the Scriptures is their inexhaustibility. It's not outdated. It's still the struggle that is going on. And therefore I affirm the validity of wrestling with the word, and it seems to me that smaller group meetings are important for this. If nothing else happens in those meetings, there has at least been rapport, with three or five people saying: "What is that Scripture really saying? I just don't understand, I didn't understand that before." So, I'd say that that is a key element for my understanding of worship. It is wrestling with the word.

The egoic interpretation sees the worshiper as an actor partly receiving and partly producing the ritual symbols and activities. A friend who was used to mass ritual put it this way:

> We really both had a great time. You know, it was two hours, and we weren't aware that the time had passed at all. But I sense that it couldn't be a steady diet for us. For one thing, I got the feeling that would just be too exhausting. That there, *the whole depended on what everyone was*

FIGURE 6. Chalkboard Diagram

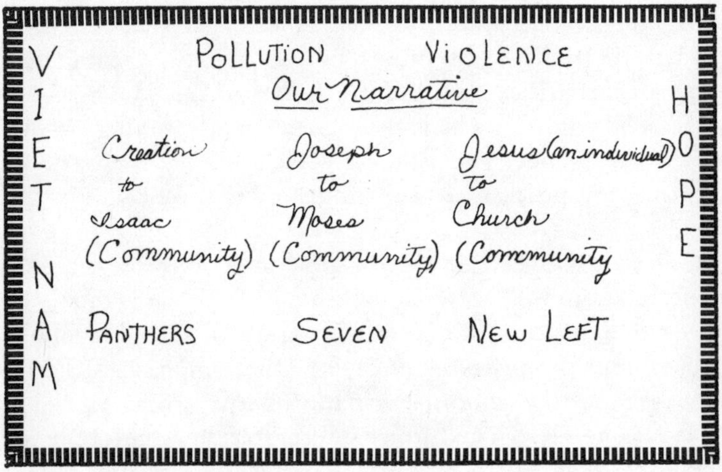

V	POLLUTION	VIOLENCE		
I	*Our Narrative*			**H**
E	*Creation*	*Joseph*	*Jesus (an individual)*	**O**
T	*to*	*to*	*to*	**P**
	Isaac	*Moses*	*Church*	**E**
N	*(Community)*	*(Community)*	*(Community)*	
A	PANTHERS	SEVEN	NEW LEFT	
M				

contributing. And you were never just watching. You were participating, and it took a lot of energy.[6]

Another example of the egoic interpretation is a sermon I heard at the Church of the Three Crosses. For this worship service, a chalkboard was set up in the church, containing the diagram presented in figure 6. The sermon developed the idea that we must rehearse our story but, beyond that, we must minister to one another in making decisions, because it is in making decisions that "our narrative," which is the "ground of your being," is made a part of the world.

The meaning of the ritual, according to this interpretation, is that it is a forum in which the group acts to specify the meaning of the sacred cosmos by specifying the relationship between "our narrative" and the events constituting the secular world. This interpretation of ritual requires egoic activity: interpretation, ethical decisions, and feedback.

A psychological interpretation of this view of ritual is that it values cultivation of contact with unconscious knowledge and de-

[6] From a transcribed interview with a lay person. (Emphasis added.) The habitual participants in interaction ritual—those who voice the egoic interpretation—find the experience cathartic and sometimes even exhilarating.

sires. The egoic interpretation says that the very essence of ritual is "wrestling." This "wrestling with *the word*" is a personal struggle to articulate meanings. The source of these meanings is perceived as manifold: partly in traditional symbols, but also equally within one's self. Each person's intuitive contribution is part of the final meaning of the rite. The "whole" (which means the final meaning of this worship service) does indeed depend on what everyone is contributing. In fact, the very process of "contribution" is the essence of the ritual.   summary →anonym and egoism

Thus, these two exegeses of ritual—egoic and objective—emphasize different relationships between worshipers and the symbols of the sacred. One emphasizes the external nature of sacred symbols, emanating from one's "environment." The other emphasizes the internal source of sacred symbols, emanating partly from "outside" and partly from one's self. The former interpretation therefore tends to make believers dependent on sources of meaning outside themselves. Such sources of meaning are in the first instance religious experts and specialists. Thus this interpretation tends to value religious institutions such as hierarchy and tradition. The latter interpretation tends to make religious believers "autonomous." Inasmuch as self is the source of symbols and meanings, all believers are equal. Institutional sources of meaning diminish in importance. The process of discovering meaning becomes central to the group's religious behavior.

THE OPERATIONAL MEANING: MASS RITUAL AND INTERACTION RITUAL

The operational meaning of ritual is contained in the motor activities performed in the course of ritual (for example, processions, bowing, sitting, handling of objects) and in that aspect of language known as style (especially the distinction between archaic and contemporary linguistic styles). Insofar as motor activity is performed by assigned actors, the operational meaning includes the role patterns of ritual performance. The question is not only what motor activity is performed but also who does what—who speaks and who listens, and, if all speak, who initiates utterances and who responds.

The operational meanings of our four rituals are consistent with their exegetical meanings. In general, rituals whose exegesis is objective use motor activities structured by hierarchical roles and also

distinguish rigorously between "sacred" and "secular" modes of
activity. Rituals whose interpretation is egoic have fluid role structures and include many "secular" elements in their repertoires of
activities appropriate to ritual. These operational differences result
in overall differences between two kinds of ritual. In rituals of objective exegesis, lay people appear to be culturally passive.[7] They act in
unison, as a mass, in response to the initiation and direction of clergy.
Hence we call this form mass ritual. In rituals of egoic interpretation,
the participants interact with one another as equals and also interact
with their traditional symbols—changing them as well as being changed
by them. Hence we call this form interaction ritual.

[7] By "culturally passive" I mean abstaining from the creation of new symbol
systems. I have no evidence to show that passivity-dependence is a general personality trait of participants in mass ritual as contrasted to participants in interaction ritual. In fact, the opposite is true. Those who accept an "objective"
interpretation of ritual may be passive in church, but they are active outside of
church. Moreover, although they do not express disagreement in the ritual, they
frequently disagree privately, and they select from the ritual and the sermon
what they find supportive and reject what they think is incorrect or inapplicable.
    A pastor who presides at a mass ritual called this to my attention by asking:
"Are you saying, then, that participation of members of the Body of Christ . . .
in the formation of a foundling home, a home for the aged, a new home for con-
valescents, their benevolent giving, which are the highest of any congregation in
our tradition in the United States, support for low-income housing, legal aid, en-
gagement in peace action, and other expressions of mission are the fruit of the
congregation's passivity or an aberration of some kind?"
    Such activity may well be perfectly congruent with "cultural passivity." That
is, within the scope of a traditional religious symbol system, there is a wide range
of social activities legitimized by that symbol system. The performance of those
activities is based on the accepted meaningfulness of the religious system.
    Therefore, what we have in the difference between mass ritual and interac-
tion ritual is not so much a psychological difference or process as a cultural process. It is not even a specifically "religious" difference, in that participants in one
kind of ritual are more or less faithful, devout, or principled in their social actions. But the participants in interaction ritual see the need for revising a symbol
system. This is the revision of culture, insofar as culture itself is a system of
symbols and the meanings which they define.
    The evidence for speaking of "cultural passivity" comes entirely from the
assumption that the "operational meaning" of ritual is in fact a *meaning*. The
fact, therefore, that participants in mass ritual behave differently in church from
participants in interaction ritual—even if there were to be no other behavioral
difference—is interpretable. Moreover, as the following pages will show, taking
part in interaction ritual requires the expenditure of much energy, arouses strong
emotions, any leads to the cultivation of conflict and to introspection and self-
criticism.
    The conclusion seems to be that the creation of a symbol system is a specific
cultural process, and in interaction ritual we have evidence that there are active
as well as passive stances toward this activity.

The handling of the sacred symbols includes the manipulation of the segments and operations of the ritual scenario. There is variance in the degree to which participants in ritual create or eliminate segments, rearrange their order, and change their titles. There is variance in the degree to which participants add or drop operations, rearrange their order, modify their content or linguistic and musical style, or specify the roles of actor/initiator and reactor/receiver of the sacred utterances or actions expressed in the operations.

Mass ritual is characterized by (1) distinct clergy and laity roles in the performance of ritual, a distinction which is usually indicated by clothing, but whose essential property is the initiation of sacred utterance or action; (2) tradition-prescribed or clergy-prescribed titles of segments, sequences of segments, and sequence, content, and style of operations; (3) archaic linguistic style and the use of the organ as the predominant ritual musical instrument. These three basic characteristics give rise to the phenomenon of uniform behavior of the lay participants in ritual. That is, lay persons perform reactive utterances and behavior in unison.

Interaction ritual is characterized by the opposite properties: (1) lack of distinction between the roles of clergy and of laity in the performance of ritual;[8] (2) group selection of the elements of ritual, including segments and their titles and sequence, and operations and their number, titles, sequence, content, and style; (3) the inclusion of contemporary linguistic and musical styles. (Traditional styles are included as well, in order to provide a sense of continuity with the past, but are given slightly less than equal place in the ritual.) These characteristics give rise to the phenomenon of multiplex roles among the participants in the performance of ritual. This means, in concrete terms, that at any given moment in any given ritual, it is impossible to predict who is going to speak or initiate action next.

THE ROLES OF CLERGY AND LAITY

In mass ritual the roles of clergy and laity are distinct. The essential expression of this distinction in the performance of ritual is the initiation of utterance or action. This investiture of power in a special

[8] There is still distinction of roles based on technical skills. That is, speakers give speeches, musicians play and sing, artists make banners and do decorations. But none of these distinctions is based on the assumption of differential access to the correct or official meaning of the ritual.

class of actors in the ritual is typically indicated by the use of special clothing and by the structure of the procession which begins the ritual performance.

In respect to clothing, the issue is not the degree of elaboration but the sheer fact of its distinctiveness. The complex and elaborate vestments of the priest in the Roman Catholic ritual indicate a recognition of ancient cultural heritage, but they do not perform the function of distinguishing the clergy from the laity any more completely than the more simple robes, stoles, or collars of the Protestant clergy. Distinctive clothes *set apart*.

In the rituals under discussion, three use distinctive clothing and one does not. In the rituals of St. Paul, St. Clement, and St. James these vestments are, respectively: an ankle-length black robe and a collar in the shape of the two stone tablets of the Mosaic law; the chasuble, maniple, stole, cincture, alb, and amice of the priestly vestments; and a surplice. In the ritual of the Church of the Three Crosses, the minister wears "street dress," which varies according to the weather from suit and tie to sport clothes *sans* coat or tie.

PROCESSIONS

All four rituals have processions, but their operational properties vary significantly. Of the ritual procession, G. Van der Leeuw has observed:

> The *procession* is an elementary dance and fulfills the purpose of mobilizing the cult community, that is, the sacred common element, of activating power; and every procession is as it were a sacramental procession, so far as it sets something sacred in motion and extends its powerfulness over a certain region. . . . Fundamentally the procession is a circuit, whether it wanders about the village or the town, or makes an actual circle around an object, a field or a house, etc. It restricts and concentrates power. . . .[9]

The most elaborate procession occurs in St. Paul, accompanied by a "processional hymn." The order of procession is that the least "sacred" actors go first and the more sacred actors in successive positions behind them. The usual sequence of participants would then be: lay readers, the choir, any assisting clergy, and finally the presiding clergyman. The choir wear ankle-length red robes to indicate that they have donned a special relationship to the dynamics of ritual.

[9] G. Van der Leeuw, *Religion in Essence and Manifestation* (New York: Harper and Row, Torchbooks, 1961), p. 377.

The clergy are also robed. The procession is staged in the back of the church, in an area behind the pews for the lay participants in the ritual. It moves with the rhythm of the music up the center aisle to the chancel,[10] where the respective participants move to their assigned places. The persons in the procession sing as they move, and although the lay participants are also encouraged to sing, their contribution is usually weak since they have not practiced.

In the ritual of St. Clement, the procession is simpler. It includes the presiding clergyman and the young men or boys who assist in the ritual as acolytes. The procession forms in a dressing room out of sight and moves from there to the altar, with acolytes preceding the presiding clergyman.[11] The acolytes are, as a rule, robed in ankle-length black robes and surplices. During the procession, the organ plays or the congregation sings. The congregation is assembled in the pews before the procession begins, and each person stands in place during the movement of the "celebrant" and the acolytes.

In the ritual of St. James, the minister enters the chancel from the adjacent sacristy after the congregation is assembled in the pews. The congregation stands to meet him. This is the simplest of all the processions we have observed, but it is still an entrance of a special class of person. Although it is only a vestigial procession, it is still a processional movement limited to one, power-bearing segment of the congregation.

In the Church of the Three Crosses, the procession includes all the members of the congregation. When the time for beginning the ritual arrives, the members are generally gathered in small informal groups, conversing, drinking coffee, taking off their coats, and so on. Some may be on the second floor of the building or in the sanctuary, some

[10] The full description of the various spatial divisions in the churches of our study and their meaning will be given below when we discuss positional meaning. However, it should be explained now that the Protestant room for worship is typically divided into chancel and sanctuary. The sanctuary is the whole room, and the chancel is that part of the sanctuary which is raised above the floor level of the whole, is in front of the ritual space, and is the area in which the activities of the ritual are performed, as on a stage.

In Roman Catholic churches, similar spatial divisions have different labels. The raised area in which the ritual is performed is called the sanctuary, and the larger, lower area where lay people stay is called the nave.

One of the important differences between mass ritual and interaction ritual, as we have noted previously, is the permeability of these boundaries between more and less sacred zones within the house of worship.

[11] Processions in more solemn Roman Catholic rituals—such as Easter services and rites at which a bishop presides—have the same order of participants as in St. Paul Church.

downstairs in the hall or kitchen, and, in good weather, some outside on the front steps or sidewalk. The organist begins playing as a signal that persons should assemble. When the music begins, they move—often continuing their conversations—toward the stairs and toward the sanctuary. They break off their conversations gradually. Among the persons who move up the stairs and into the sanctuary in this informal way is the minister who is to preside at the service. He moves with the other members of the congregation and takes his place in a front pew—not visibly distinguished from any other pew in the sanctuary. When the organist sees that everyone is assembled and quiet, he plays for a moment longer, and then the first verbal operation of the ritual is initiated.

All four of these rituals also employ another procession, the offertory procession. In the Roman Catholic ritual, this is the action of presenting the elements of bread and wine to be used in the eucharistic ritual and, along with these gifts for the eucharist, the material gifts (principally money, but sometimes gifts in kind) for the support of the clergy and of church activities. In the Protestant ritual, the offertory is included in the Response to the Word segment of the ritual. Although it has a distant relation to the eucharistic meal, this connection is less emphasized.

In all four rituals, the offertory procession is the action in which lay persons make a symbolic (and real) contribution to the "work of the church" and therefore to God. In gratitude and respect for the spiritual nourishment of the sacred word, members of the church respond with gifts.

One usual form of the offertory procession in mass ritual is that after the ushers have passed the collection basket or plate(s) around the congregation, they gather at the back of the central aisle and then march up to the boundary between sanctuary and chancel (nave and sanctuary in St. Clement), and place the containers on the steps of the sacred stage, usually by reaching over the boundary from "their own" space without entering the sacred space. A variant is for the ushers to hand the baskets or plates to the presiding clergyman, who has come down to the boundary between chancel and sanctuary to accept them. The baskets are then placed on the altar table, and a hymn is sung or a prayer recited. In the Roman Catholic ritual, the money offerings are usually not used symbolically. Rather, after the collection is taken up, it is removed to the sacristy or some other safe place. The bread and wine for the eucharistic rites are, however, used symbolically. The gifts are brought in procession by two members of the congregation and handed to the priest at the boundary between nave and sanctuary.

In the interaction ritual of the Church of the Three Crosses, the procedure is fundamentally the same in that a collection is taken up and then the ushers carry the plates up the center aisle. But they place the plates on the altar table themselves. It is not correct to make a central argument of this one facet, because the difference between mass ritual and interaction ritual is cumulative over the whole series of operations in the ritual scenario. The distinctive offertory procession in this interaction ritual is significant, however. Because there is no clearly marked boundary between the sanctuary and the chancel, and so no boundary at which the ushers can stand, they place the gifts directly on the altar table.

THE DISTRIBUTION OF INITIATING ACTS

With respect to the performance of the other operations of ritual, mass ritual is characterized by extremely rare lay initiation, and this initiation is furthermore limited to the sermon and the reading/recitation of scriptures, announcements, or other structured utterances or actions. (Assisting with the distribution of communion is such an action.) In interaction ritual, by contrast, the role of initiating utterance or action is distributed throughout the congregation.

Examples of initiation of an operation would be as follows. First are the numerous short greeting-response operations, such as:

PASTOR: In the Name of the Father, and of the Son, and of the Holy Spirit.
PEOPLE: Amen.
PASTOR: The Lord Be With You.
PEOPLE: And with you also.

Second, there are operations where the content of the clerical initiation is not fully specified:

PASTOR: Assurance of Pardon.
RESPONSE (PEOPLE): All glory be to God on high, Who Hath our race befriended. . . .

Following is an example of multiplex initiation within a single operation: (The "leader" in this kind of example is, as often as not, a lay member of the congregation.)

LEADER: Lord, could you please take the time today to listen to how we feel?

RIGHT: God, I'm angry. Deep down inside me, I'm angry. Are you listening, God?

LEFT: I'm angry because people ignore me and laugh at me. They use me like a mat and treat me like a kid. Are you there, Lord?

RIGHT: (Etc.)

LEFT: (Etc.)

RIGHT: (Etc.)

Another instance of difference between analogous operations in mass ritual and in interaction ritual is the difference between the "Intercessions" in the ritual of St. Clement and the "Expression of Concerns, Joys, and Sorrows" in the ritual of the Church of the Three Crosses. The operation called Intercessions is performed as follows: The priest says, "Let us pray." Then he (or a member of the choir or a lay reader) continues by reading (or chanting on a single note) a list of issues, previously prepared by the clergy and expressed in such a way that after the statement of each issue the congregation may respond with either "Let us pray to the Lord" or "We pray to the Lord." (Where there are lay "liturgical teams" in Roman Catholic congregations, preparation of these issues for intercession is one of the tasks they perform.) There follows a moment of silent prayer. Then the celebrant concludes, "We ask this through Christ Our Lord," and the congregation answers, "Amen."

The operation called Expression of Concerns, Joys, and Sorrows proceeds as follows. The minister presiding over the ritual says: "Now it is time to express our Concerns, Joys, and Sorrows which we have experienced during the past week." A silence of varying length follows as the participants gather their thoughts. Then follow personal statements (from three to eleven in the rituals I observed) by various members of the congregation in their own words. For example: "I would like to express a concern for Mrs. Smith, who fell down and broke her hip. If anyone wants to visit her, she is in Room 352 at Grant Hospital." "For people who slam doors on precinct workers." "I'd like to welcome the Joneses back from Wyoming." Also at this time extended statements are made which embody concern about current events (such as the war in Vietnam or the violent demonstrations) or accounts of difficulties at work or in the family. In addition, a speaker may be asked to clarify his or her concern during this time.

Another aspect of the differences between mass ritual and interaction ritual in the distribution of the role of initiation is the occurrence of impromptu utterances by lay participants. In mass ritual, such an occurrence is considered highly unusual and disruptive, an indication that the structure of unconscious bonds of the congregation has been violated. In one of the congregations under consideration, such an impromptu utterance occurred during a sermon by a "liberal" pastor after the demonstrations at the Democratic National Convention. In the sermon, the pastor referred to the Chicago police as "Keystone Cops." The exact content of the lay person's comment has not been recorded, but the event of the outburst, made during the sermon, was remembered and recounted with some awe two years after its occurrence. In the interaction ritual of the Church of the Three Crosses, I myself observed four such utterances by lay persons. In none of these instances did the person who made the comment leave, nor are such comments always kept track of, although it is known that certain members of the congregation are more disposed toward such contributions than others. It is considered as "their style" and accepted as a symptom of healthy community interest in the content of the service.

The distinction between clerical and lay roles in the initiation of sacred utterances and sacred actions is contained in the *customs* relevant to such roles. In mass ritual, there is some lay initiation, but this is not usual, and in most cases it is highly unusual. There are special occasions and special lay persons. In interaction ritual the minister still initiates many ritual operations, it is usual for any lay participant to perform such initiation of operations.

THE SELECTION OF THE ELEMENTS OF RITUAL

In mass ritual the selection of the elements of the ritual is prescribed either by tradition (which may be either denominational or local) or by clergymen. This applies to the selection and labeling of the segments and operations and the content of operations.

Lay persons have various degrees of autonomy in the selection of these elements in mass ritual, but their freedom does not include the selection of any and all elements, as is the case in interaction ritual. One kind of freedom given to lay liturgy teams and worship and sacrament committees is to choose the content of certain operations of the ritual from officially provided repertoires. These repertoires are usually printed in sources emanating from the official liturgical committee of the denomination.

Often lay persons select the musical forms to be used in the ritual. Organists, choir directors, and other musicians work with the pastor in choosing songs and other musical pieces. One of the churches, St. Paul, has had a tradition of performing polyphonic choral arrangements of introits, some of them original compositions by St. Paul's choir director. (It is also the case, however, that these musicians were salaried specialists, not necessarily members of the congregation.)

In interaction ritual the selection of elements is entrusted to lay persons. Usually a group works with the pastor to construct interaction ritual. The pastor does not dominate the activity of the group as the specialist whose opinion is authoritative. He may perform as a resource person, who in this case is familiar with scholarly commentaries on the Bible. But the activity of the group centers on the task of hearing and considering the feelings and intuitions of all members of the group, however orthodox or unorthodox those feelings and intuitions may be. A remark often heard in such a group, in reference to a particular passage from the Bible, is: "Well, that just doesn't grab me." Such comments are taken, not as confessions of ignorance, but as judgments on the authenticity or the meaningfulness of the scriptural passage. Such comments generally lead to a discussion which seeks to find a common ground between the meaning expressed in the sacred text and the meaning contained in the emotions and intuitions of the participants.

Although the scriptural passages used in interaction ritual are usually taken from a sequential repertoire,[12] on one occasion I participated in a group which discarded passages from Isaiah and the Letter to the Romans in favor of a poem by Denise Levertov ("The Muse") as the sacred text for the Sunday ritual. This is not an uncommon occurrence in the construction of interaction ritual.

The range of choices in such a group includes all the elements of ritual: content of operations, sequence of operations, titles and order and content of segments. The initial question for such groups is on the order of, "Well, what shall we do next Sunday?" Such a group often gets into a long discussion of the members' most personal ideas, attitudes, and feelings concerning religion and ritual. Divergent and even contrary understandings frequently arise. Although attempts

[12] A sequential repertoire is a published list of pericopes of the Bible. Pericopes are unit-segments of the biblical narrative determined by scholars who have figured out that the Bible is composed of narratives that were transmitted orally before they were written down. Each pericope contains an integral story, incident, or comment. Catholic churches use an annual sequence of pericopes; that is, they "cover" the whole Bible in one year. Other denominations publish recommended weekly readings which repeat themselves only every two years or even every seven years.

are made to resolve such differences, when resolution is not possible, the participants agree to disagree and, furthermore, to construct a ritual which does not express one of two or more contrary positions but rather expresses the common concern of all to continue to wrestle through the meaning of the disputed passage.

STYLE: LANGUAGE AND MUSIC

Mass ritual tends to use archaic and formal linguistic styles; the use of informal language (for example, slang) is exceptional. Interaction ritual regularly uses informal language, including slang. It also uses formal language, but the use of archaisms is exceptional.

This difference in linguistic style can best be exemplified by citing analogous operations in the four rituals we are examining. The operation is the address to the Deity, which occurs early in all four rituals. The operation has various titles: Call to Worship, Invocation, Collect, General Prayer. The following are the typical forms of this operation:

1. In St. James:
Almighty and everlasting God, who art worthy to be had in reverence by all the children of men, we give Thee most humble and hearty thanks for the innumerable blessings, both temporal and spiritual, which, without any merit or worthiness on our part, Thou hast bestowed upon us.

We praise Thee especially that Thou hast preserved unto us in their purity Thy saving Word and the sacred ordinances of Thy house. . . .

The prayer is quite long, and uses the archaic pronouns and verb forms throughout.

2. In St. Paul:
Almighty God, help us now by Thy grace and power to cast away the works of darkness and put on the armor of light, that on the last day when our Lord shall come to judge us we may have a future and a hope. Through Him who lives and reigns with Thee and the Holy Spirit now and forever. Amen.

3. In St. Clement:
Let us pray. Our Lord watch over your household with constant loving care. Let your protection forever shield those who rely solely upon the help of your heavenly grace. We ask you this through our Lord Jesus Christ, your son, who lives and reigns with you and the Holy Spirit, one God, forever and ever.

ALL: Amen.

4. In the Church of the Three Crosses:
O Lord, we seldom see ourselves honestly. Maybe it's too painful or may-

be we don't want to take the time. But we do know that we let the broken-
ness of life overshadow the eternal wholeness. We fail to transmit life from
the source of life itself.

Renew us! Fill us with joy. Let us dance with Snoopy, sing with Pete
Seeger, and shout with our brother man for joy. Amen!

The first two prayers use the archaic forms of the second-person
pronoun to address the Deity. The third prayer (from the Roman
Catholic ritual) has dispensed with those archaisms. The fourth has
dispensed not only with archaisms but also with formal modes of
speech and has moved into the casual language characteristic of
everyday speech. This prayer also introduces into the sacred address
references to a comic-strip character and a folksinger. These secular
references are inconceivable in the styles of the other three forms of
sacred address.

The variations in the musical styles of mass ritual and interaction
ritual appear to be variations in the *range* of styles used. The range
of musical styles available to worshipers is as follows:

1. Traditional, sacred, virtuoso (motets, polyphony)
2. Traditional, sacred, popular (traditional hymns)
3. Contemporary, sacred, popular
4. Contemporary, secular, popular

The majority of the pieces of music used in mass ritual are of the
first two kinds, with occasional use of the third. The majority of
songs and pieces used in interaction ritual are taken from the fourth
and third, with occasional use of the second and rare use of the first.

Since I am not an expert in the psychology of music, I shall omit
detailed discussion of the nuances of musical genre which may help
to explain this variation in musical repertoires. However, such nuances
do seem to be of considerable importance. (Habitual participants in
interaction ritual find the music of mass ritual "dull" and "somber,"
while habitual participants in mass ritual find the musical style of
interaction ritual "distracting" and "lacking in dignity.")

There is another factor that goes to explain this variance, which is
more properly sociological and concerning which data do exist. One
informant comments:

> I remember some of the first reactions in regard to the hymns that were
> used, which were pretty bad. I mean to the content of the old hymnal.
> There aren't too many hymns that really gather up a theology of the cruci-
> form understanding, the suffering servant, embracing the world, living joy-
> fully. There's so much of the individualism and the isolation of the hymns
> that it was really hard to have them be an integral part of the service with-

out them being somehow some separate segment of the service. . . . Even in an informal, nonliturgical way, people gather together and start singing songs—songs, you know, that reflect something about their understanding. So, in the civil rights movement, the songs are very much hymns: they reflected the battles, the times of understanding they have. But none of the hymns, the music, we have do that. They reflect a different age, a different understanding. It does not reflect who we are at this point. This music certainly does not reflect any of the urban images . . . very rural-oriented symbols and all that. I think there's one hymn in there, "Praise to Thee, O God, for Cities." It was written in 1956 by a guy who went to the same seminary we did. So we taught them that. I remember shortly after we got here, there was at least one hymn that dealt with the cities.

Interaction ritual seeks music which expresses "who we are at this point"—that is, the egoic definition of the sacred. The sacred is, in this context, "our" deepest feelings about or ultimate explanations of everyday social experience. From the repertoire of music used in the interaction ritual we have observed most closely, it is clear that this music must deal not only with the city but with all social experience. There are some songs which become regularly repeated "standards" for interaction ritual. These account for approximately 90 percent of the songs used in a twelve-month period. The rest of the songs used are used only once, or a very few times, as long as their popularity lasts. But this repertoire is never fixed; it always remains open to whatever may authentically express the feelings of the congregation at any given point.[13]

The use of music is extremely varied in interaction ritual. Usually the whole congregations sings, but if the song is new or difficult, solos are performed. Often a recording is played, and the congregation will listen, or sing along to the best of its ability.

Mass ritual and interaction ritual differ more in the repertoires used than in the musical instruments used, but it is also true that the organ accompanies almost all the songs in the first two repertoires, whereas the guitar frequently accompanies songs in the last two. However, the organ is also an instrument for rock music. I have heard it used as such in interaction ritual, for the "organ postlude," and also for the "silent meditation" after the sermon.[14]

[13] The most frequently used "standard" in the Church of the Three Crosses is a traditional Shaker hymn, with new words by an unknown author. The original title of the song was "Simple Gifts." The melody has been used as thematic material by Aaron Copeland in his *Appalachian Spring*. The version used in the Church of the Three Crosses is called "The Lord of the Dance." Some of the songs used only once or a few times during their secular popularity are "Good Morning Starshine," a Pepsi-Cola commercial, and "Jesus Is a Soul Man."

[14] The organist in this case was the kind of musician who could exist only in

We should also point out the "faddist" or syncretistic use of the guitar in mass ritual. Because the guitar symbolizes being up-to-date, it is sometimes brought into mass ritual without congregational participation. I have seen this in the ritual of one church, in which the guitarist acts as an official of the ceremony, standing apart from the worshipers, announces what is to be sung, and plays and sings virtually as a soloist, with the weak accompaniment of the congregation.

TWO DISTINCTIVE OPERATIONS: THE TALKBACK AND THE SECULAR READING

The ritual of the Church of the Three Crosses includes two operations which are distinctive to interaction ritual. The talkback follows immediately after the organ postlude of the standard ritual scenario. Its purpose is to encourage the members of the congregation to respond not only to the sermon but to the whole ritual just performed. This feedback session was begun ostensibly to provide for continuous resolution of the different ritual styles of the two congregations which merged in 1965 to form the Church of the Three Crosses. During the first few months of the merger, the talkback was well attended and actively participated in by most members of the new congregation. Since that time, this institutionalized feedback has gone through cycles of dormancy and activity. The dormant talkback is one in which there is no single focus of the whole group's discussion; rather, the members of the congregation break up into groups of two, three, or four and engage in small talk and animated conversation about topics of personal interest to the participants. This is done over coffee, which is provided in the office of the church.[15] The

---

a ritual open to the integration of sacred and secular worlds. He is a nineteen-year-old music student who does not share the religious background of the congregation (the church is Protestant, the organist Catholic). He brings a highly egoic style of music to the ritual in that he plays all preludes, recessionals, and meditation music not only by ear but ad libitum—that is, making it up as he goes along, on the inspiration of the moment. The congregation thus routinely hears motifs ranging from Bach to the Rolling Stones. Although there has been minor friction between the organist and the congregation over his reluctance to play written musical accompaniments to traditional hymns, this issue has been resolved by compromise: the congregation sings some of those hymns a capella, and the organist sometimes plays the accompaniment. This resolution grows out of mutual respect for the authenticity of the congregation's style, on the one hand, and the improvisational skills of the organist, on the other.

[15] For a diagram of the spatial divisions in the Church of the Three Crosses, see figure 9, p. 126. The office is the section labeled "E."

cycle of dormancy and activity is governed by the congregation's own sense of crisis. During the demonstrations in 1968 and the fall of 1969, and during the trial of the "Conspiracy Seven" in Chicago, the talkback was quite active. Talkbacks are also generated by individual members of the congregation who announce that they have something they want to discuss about the sermon, the worship service, or elements of ritual. One such discussion involved criticism of the song which begins: "They will know that we are Christians by our love." The point of the criticism was that it is arrogant to think that Christians are known by their love, for in fact they are not. Therefore, the criticism went, the words should be "They will know that we are human by our love." There was disagreement on this issue, and the resolution was to discontinue singing that particular song. (After the member of the congregation who voiced the criticism moved away and was no longer able to come to church regularly, the congregation began to sing the song again occasionally.) Another such discussion involved criticism of the "Prayer of Dedication," which had been in use in the congregation for more than two years. It occurred as an operation immediately following the offering of gifts, in the segment entitled Response to the Word. Its text is:

> We accept, O Lord, the whole world, its people, its structures, its joys, its sorrows, as our responsibility. Now receive the offering of our lives, a living sacrifice, that with Thee we may promote peace and humanness among all men and within all structures. Through Jesus Christ Our Lord. Amen.[16]

A worship task force set up a ritual in which the Prayer of Dedication was the introductory operation, and the rest of the ritual was a commentary on the prayer. The basis of the criticism was that the prayer is unrealistic, in that this congregation could not be responsible for the whole world, only for that part of the world with which it has real contact.

As a consequence of this criticism, the Prayer of Dedication was dropped from the ritual. After several weeks, its place was taken by

[16] This prayer comes from the liturgy of the Ecumenical Institute in Chicago. EI, as it is often called, is a Protestant monastic community founded in the late 1950s. Its members are single men and women and married couples whose children are included in the scope of monastic life. The members of EI sing a monastic office daily and accept a common rule and discipline. They travel throughout the United States giving lectures and theology classes to church groups. They also conduct training sessions for clergy. The co-pastors of the Church of the Three Crosses attended such a session together during the summer of 1964.

a new prayer, composed by the members of another worship task force. The text of the new prayer is:

> Christ has many services to be done; some are easy, others are difficult. Some bring honor, others bring reproach. Some are suitable to our natural inclinations and temporal interests, others are contrary to both. In some we may please Christ and please ourselves, in others we cannot please Christ except by denying ourselves. Yet the power to do all these things is assuredly given us in Christ, who strengthens us. Amen.

egoism

The talkback is a clear manifestation of the conscious bonds of unity in this group of believers. The "alliance of autonomous egos" is manifested in energetic debate, the attempt to arrive at substantive agreements, and the agreement to disagree. The controversy in these discussions is often heated but rarely fractious.

Some individuals have stopped attending services at the Church of the Three Crosses because of different understandings which have emerged in the talkback, but these departures were not marked by the anger typical of departures from congregations which have no form of institutionalized feedback. Nor were such disagreements with the preacher (or the worship task force, or the congregation's traditions) marked by the characteristics of the "revolt against the leader" described by Slater.[17] Defensiveness stemming from threatened ego-loss did not occur in this forum in the two years of my participation.

The "secular reading" is another operation distinctive to interaction ritual. This operation involves reading a passage from some source considered secular. Its position in the ritual is immediately before or after the "sacred reading." The use of this operation in the Church of the Three Crosses began in July 1965, with a reading from Dag Hammarskjöld's *Markings*. Among Unitarians in the United States, it is more customary to use such secular readings than it is to use readings from the Bible, but the impact of placing a contemporary reading immediately next to a traditionally sacred text is different from the exclusion of traditionally sacred texts in favor or secular sources of meaning.

In one instance in the ritual of the Church of the Three Crosses, these two texts were called "The Ancient Word" and "The Contemporary Word." "Word" in this idiom means a sacred utterance, and the labels thus signify perception of the sacred in contemporary events and utterances as well as in past events and utterances. This

[17] Philip E. Slater, *Microcosm: Structural, Psychological and Religious Evolution in Groups* (New York: John Wiley, 1966), chapter 2.

means that sacredness is not in a set of fixed symbols but in a process of perceiving and interpretation. What makes the text sacred is its meaning, and the meaning is discovered by the person who perceives (reads or hears) the utterance or event in question. Meaning is not "given" but arises from conscious processes of perception and interpretation.

The implication of this juxtaposition is that the Bible is to be handled interactively, just as one handles contemporary wakeful experience of social reality. On the other hand, contemporary social reality is to be handled as one handles the Bible, seriously and with the expectation of discovering ultimate meaning. The place of meaning thus shifts from the *percept* (the sacred text) to the perceiving subject and to a process of wakeful attention to and perception of inner and outer reality, "self" as well as "environment."

The use of the secular reading, therefore, is symbolic of the extreme permeability of the boundary between the sacred and profane worlds. Psychically, the worshiper is situated precisely on that boundary, and so both worlds—sacred and profane—are perceived as impinging on and emanating from the self. The use of a series of secular readings sets the individual self in the context of other, equally autonomous selves. These other selves constitute "community," and the process of extruding the sacred cosmos from the inarticulate realm of unconscious intuitions into conscious, articulated symbols and institutions is the ongoing concern of this community. This process is operationalized by discussion and debate and by trial-and-error experimentation with new songs, symbols, and operations of ritual and critical reflection on their conformity to the basic intuitions of the congregation.

THE POSITIONAL MEANING

The positional meaning of ritual is the set of relationships indicated by the spatial setting of the ritual. Mass ritual and interaction ritual are sharply distinguished by different spatial arrangements. Mass ritual takes place in a setting which has two clearly marked zones: the more sacred zone, in which the ritual action takes place, and a less sacred zone ("profane" in relation to the stage on which the ritual is enacted, "sacred" in relation to the world outside the building).

Interaction ritual is characterized not by an absence of distinction between more and less sacred zones in the ritual space but by more permeable boundaries between those two zones. It is performed in a space characterized by a permeable center of low salience.

The basic floor plan of the Protestant churches in Lincoln Park is the well-known "meeting hall with a stage" (see figure 7). The basic floor plan of the Roman Catholic Church is a cruciform room (see figure 8).

These two floor plans have different cultural roots. The Protestant design originates in the idea of the congregation as a community similar to the civil communities of small towns. The Catholic plan is more directly reminiscent of the death of Jesus, shaped as it is in the form of a cross. But the two floor plans are, or can be, identical in the nature of the relationship of the central area in which the ritual is performed to the peripheral, lower area in which the lay participants/spectators of the ritual stay.

In the four rituals under consideration, three—St. Paul's, St. Clement's, and St. James's—take place in spaces marked by sharp

FIGURE 7. Common Floor Plan of a Protestant Church

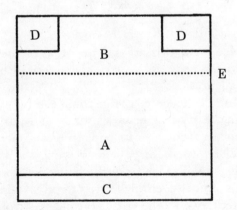

A—The Sanctuary
B—The Chancel
C—The Vestibule
D—Sacristies and Workrooms
E—The Boundary between Chancel
   and Sanctuary

FIGURE 8. Common Floor Plan of a Roman Catholic Church

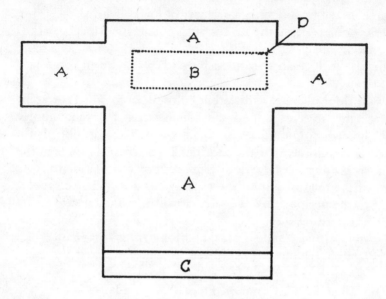

A—The Nave   C—The Vestibule
B—The Sanctuary   D—The Altar Railing

differentiation between the two areas. The ritual of the Church of the Three Crosses takes place in a space characterized by a permeable center of low salience.

In St. Paul the worship space is a large room (96 by 60 feet) with a high vaulted ceiling. Fifty-two pews are fixed in a position in the sanctuary, twenty-six on each side of a wide (6 feet) center aisle. The floor of the chancel is raised thirty inches above the floor of the sanctuary and ten feet in distance from the first pew. An elaborately paneled and carved pulpit is even higher (its floor is 46 inches above the floor of the sanctuary), to the left of the chancel from the point of view of the lay person in the sanctuary. Besides the pulpit, the chancel contains the organ console, tiered pews for the choir, and special seats for a presiding clergyman and two other clergy. It also contains an altar table, set against the back wall of the chancel. The movement of the ritual takes place—except for the initial and offertory processions and recessional march—entirely within this space. In fact, except for the offertory, the presiding clergyman is the only one who engages in any locomotion throughout the ritual. (Lay participants sit and stand in their places in the pews.) He moves among four places of varying degrees of sacredness. The least sacred of these is a seat built into the choir pews, where the pastor sits when some other person or group is the central focus of the ritual (for example, when the choir is singing or the lay reader is reading scripture or announcements). The second place is in the middle of the chancel, where he stands facing the people. This place is for practical instructions to the congregation and the final blessing. The third place is in the pulpit, which he occupies for the sermon. The fourth place is at the altar, which symbolizes the presence of God among the people. He moves to the altar (away from the congregation) to recite collects. These are prayers which gather up the intentions of the congregation and present those wishes and desires to God.

During this ritual, there is no crossing of the boundary between sanctuary and chancel,[18] and all initiation of sacred utterance or action comes from the chancel. The responses of the congregation from the sanctuary are in unison.

Likewise, in the rituals of St. Clement and St. James there is no crossing of the boundary between sanctuary and chancel (for St. Clement, between nave and sanctuary) during the ritual, and the initiation of sacred utterance comes from the sacred stage. All three of these mass rituals differ in many details reflecting denominational or local theologies or traditions, but they are the same in their positional meaning. They all limit the origin of sacred utterance and action to a space set aside and put lay participants in a less sacred zone, clearly marked, in which behavior is predominantly immobile and passive or directly reactive to the ritual action taking place up front.

In 1965 the ritual space of the Church of the Three Crosses was arranged in the same way as the ritual spaces of the other three churches, as a "meeting hall with a stage." On the stage (that is, in the chancel), which was raised up (20 inches higher than the sanctuary) and separated from the sanctuary by a low railing, were to be found an altar table, a pulpit for the sermon, a lectern for the sacred readings, and two special chairs for the presiding and assisting clergy-

[18] There are two exceptions to this rule. During the rite of confirmation, the young people to be confirmed—specially dressed for the occasion—cross the boundary and kneel on a prie-dieu to recite their part of the ritual. On Palm Sunday, 1971, the children of the congregation's church school formed part of the initial procession and moved into the area just inside the chancel to stage a short play dramatizing the entry of Jesus into Jerusalem. After presenting their play, they left the service.

men. The sixteen pews in the sanctuary were all arranged facing the chancel, with eight on each side of a center aisle. However, as a result of a series of changes in the congregation (described in detail in chapter 6), the ritual space in the Church of the Three Crosses was rearranged in the manner shown in figure 9.

For those who would tend to say that physical arrangements of

FIGURE 9. Floor Plan of the Church of the Three Crosses

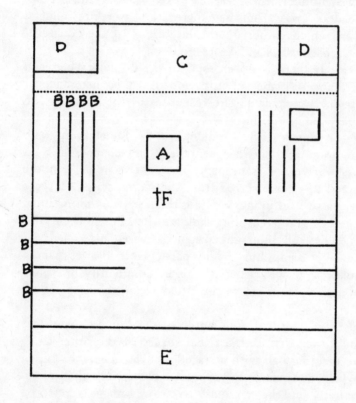

A—Altar Table   D—Sacristies and Workrooms
B—Benches   E—Vestibule and Office
C—Fallow Space   F—The Cross

space limit the possibilities of groups to symbolize their actual beliefs, this rearrangement is a striking example of the dominance of
symbolic structures over physical arrangements. The former chancel
in the Church of the Three Crosses is now "fallow" space; the current theology of this congregation has no regular use for it. Therefore, it is swept clean; the old pulpit and lectern remain fixed to the
old railing, and decorative symbols have been painted on the bare
white walls. But during the ritual, it is used for children's play. One
of the benefits of this plan is that, since the floor of the chancel is
higher than the sanctuary, the children can easily be seen and rescued
should they get into trouble, as happens with some regularity. It is
also out of the way of the ritual action and so does not interfere with
the attention being paid to the service.

With the altar table and cross moved from the separated chancel
into the midst of the congregation, the relation between the more
and less sacred spaces for ritual changes markedly. There is still a
center of the ritual space, but it is not treated with the same defer-
ence as in a more marked division. The presiding minister sits in the
pews with the rest of the congregation. He "crosses into" the more
sacred space to perform the task of "master of ceremonies," to
preach the sermon. He preaches while standing at the end of the altar
table nearer the old chancel, on the same level as the congregation.
The musical parts of the ritual are led by members of the congregation, from their places in the pews, who play the guitar and explain
any new songs. Typically, this congregation practices a new song
as it goes, singing it once weakly and then singing it again, and
allows a few weeks to learn the song and include it in the group's
regular repertoire. Operations such as the reading of scripture are
typically initiated from anywhere in the ritual space. Such readings
are randomly assigned to different members of the group (those with
good reading styles perform this task more frequently), or sometimes
the whole congregation reads the scripture together. When the communion rite is performed, the congregation crowds around the altar
table, and the bread and wine of communion are passed around from
person to person rather than distributed to each lay person by a
member of the clergy or a specially designated lay person. Before the
worship service, some persons may engage in informal conversation
at any place in the ritual space. And after the ritual, informal conversations begin, and some continue, while people are still at their places
or still standing close to the altar table.

CONCLUSION

The structural differences between mass ritual and interaction ritual show an overall pattern. These differences in exoteric exegesis and operational and positional meanings together create rituals that express different relationships between the participants and the symbols they handle in their rites. These differences focus on the kind and degree of separation between those elements of ritual that stand for the sacred and those that stand for the profane world. Mass ritual rigorously separates these two classes of elements. Interaction ritual leaves the distinction very vague and fluid.

We can present these differences in tabular form. Table 7 is a list of the elements of ritual grouped according to whether they stand for the sacred or for the profane. For mass ritual the line between the two columns is clear and carefully maintained. For interaction ritual, the line is wavering and frequently nonexistent.

The egoic and objective interpretations of ritual encompass all the elements in the table by giving a rationale for the nature of the line between them. The egoic interpretation says that all participants make the sacred meanings presented in ritual, and that ritual is in fact this process of creating meanings. It is therefore consistent that the clergy are not marked by special clothing, that processions are not rank-ordered, that lay persons initiate sacred utterance and actions, that slang and popular music are considered for use, and that congregational committees have control over the order of ritual. Since the symbol system is composed by all members of the group, it must include elements of lay social experience.

TABLE 7.   Elements of Ritual

Symbols of the Sacred	Symbols of the Profane
Clerical dress	Lay dress
Last in procession	First in procession
Pastor speaking in ritual	Others speaking in ritual
A Bach hymn	The Rolling Stones
Grammatic speech	Slang
Organ	Guitar
The Bible	Ray Bradbury
Front and center of ritual space	Back and edge of space

The objective interpretation says that the sacred is far away from normal human perception and so must be approached through special preparation and training. Thus the clergy—in their sacred function—are a class set apart from lay people. By reason of their being set apart in this manner they are qualified to make sacred utterance. Their clothes mark them, and the space in church in which they perform their sacred function is raised up and railed off.

The meaning of the difference between these boundary systems branches out in two directions. One direction is the nature of psychic relationships between individual worshipers and the symbols they handle. The other direction is the pattern of social relationships of members of the congregation to one another (in ritual), to their clergy, and to and other meaning-giving and moral authorities. The difference has both social and psychic meaning because it touches on the issue of the relationship of individual actors to moral authority. The central question is: where is moral authority?

The authority involved in religious systems has a specific and narrow meaning. Religious authority is *meaning-giving* authority, which differs from the pragmatic authority exercised by those institutions and persons whose right to command is derived from practical necessities, such as having traffic flow smoothly or getting the productive task accomplished. Therefore, when we say that these two kinds of ritual place authority in different "places," we refer only to the peculiar kind of authority which grounds meaning.

Mass ritual places meaning-giving authority outside the ego (in fact, outside the self) of the individual. In this ritual the individual worshiper says—exegetically, operationally, and positionally—"I do not have sacred authority." (The individual may have such authority outside of ritual, but it is still a *derived* authority, derived from his place in ritual.) Interaction ritual places this authority within the individual worshiper. Participants in this kind of ritual "say" structurally: "I have sacred authority, as much as anyone else." These different relationships between individual worshiper and sacred authority are most graphically presented by the positional meanings of the two rituals. Through acceptance of the positional meaning of mass ritual, the worshiper says, "Sacred authority is *apart from me.*" Through acceptance of the permeable center of low salience the worshiper in interaction ritual says, "Sacred authority is somehow other than me, stands in contrast to the experience of everyday life, but *is lodged within me.*"

We now turn to a description of the support institutions of mass ritual and interaction ritual. In that discussion we shall see in more detail how the social organization of the congregations which perform the rituals is congruent with the meanings of their settings and their internal structures.

CHAPTER 8

Comparative Patterns in Lincoln Park
3: The Support Institutions

The support institutions of ritual in Christian churches are those groups (such as committees) within the formal organization of the congregations or denominations whose purpose it is to compose the form, structure, or content of ritual. Since institutionalized religion in Western society is functionally differentiated from other institutional sectors of society, contributions to religious ritual are usually made by formal groups within an organized structure.

When we speak of the ritual of local congregations—rather than the large-scale, "occasional," crisis-oriented "state" rituals which occur from time to time in any society[1] —we must distinguish between the support institutions within the local group and those outside it. Mass ritual is more dependent on support institutions outside the local congregation, "above" it in a hierarchical organization, and interaction ritual is more dependent on institutions within the local group. Thus, from the structure of its support institutions, mass ritual appears more as a peripheral repetition of a centralized value system, and interaction ritual appears more as an independent center creating autonomous expressions of value.

[1] For a discussion of some examples of these societal rituals, see Robert N. Bellah, "Civil Religion in America," *Daedalus* 96 (1967): 1-9.

THE SUPPORT OF MASS RITUAL

Outside local congregations there are denominational committees of ritual experts (theologians, historians, biblical scholars, media specialists) and centralized communications institutions such as publishing houses. Of the rituals we are examining in this study, that of St. Clement is most dependent on support institutions outside the local congregation. The Roman Catholic church has a highly developed structure of official committees ranging from the Sacred Congregation of Rites—a working committee of the Curia of the pope—through local diocesan liturgical committees, to the recently established liturgy teams of local congregations. The products of the more central committees are published by Catholic publishing houses, subject to official approval by designated members or committees of the clergy. The two most general forms of such approval are the nihil obstat ("nothing stands in the way"), given by an officially appointed expert on the matter discussed in the publication, and the imprimatur ("it may be printed"), given by a bishop acting on the judgment of nihil obstat made by the clerical expert.

Within Roman Catholic congregations, liturgical teams may be formed. Their task is to choose from among the repertoires in official sources the content of each Sunday worship service. Musical repertoires available to such liturgical teams are very extensive as compared to the repertoires of the prayers of the worship service. Official sources also specify the sequence of segments of the ritual, the operations that must be included, and the behavioral form (that is, who may read, who may handle the elements of the communion, who may compose operations). This dependence on sources outside the local congregation extends in many cases to the content of the most variable operation of the ritual, the sermon. Some dioceses publish a list of specified topics for the Sundays throughout the year, and letters from the bishop or other official documents of the church are regularly read in place of sermons on Sunday.

The hierarchical corporate structure of decisions affecting the activities of local congregations in the Roman Catholic church also regularly includes fiscal matters. There is, therefore, homogeneity in the structures supporting ritual activity and the structures supporting the secular affairs of local Roman Catholic parishes.

Thus, in both ritual and secular matters, St. Clement Church is run on the model of a branch office of a large corporation. Most of the decisions about what shall be done in church and what shall be done as regards buying and selling property, hiring senior staff of the church and school, and so on are made outside the local congregation at more central offices of the larger ecclesiastical unit.[2]

When we turn to Protestant congregations, however, we find much local autonomy in secular affairs; therefore, when we examine these congregations, we must distinguish between the control and support of secular affairs and the control and support of ritual.

The three Protestant congregations studied in Lincoln Park have committees drawn from local membership which have legislative and policy control over the secular (mostly fiscal) affairs of the local congregation. These structures of local government are expressed in a set of official bylaws for the congregation. All three Protestant churches have a governing body composed either of all the members of the congregation (Three Crosses) or of those who have been elected to voting membership by existing voting members (St. Paul and St. James). These bodies usually meet four times a year to vote on major fiscal or policy issues of the congregation. One of these issues is the hiring (or firing) of the pastor. In addition to this governing body, there is a smaller body—variously called a board of elders, a church council, or by some other name—which meets more frequently, with the pastor, to implement policies approved by the governing body. This executive council usually has twelve members. From these members, the officers of the congregation are elected: president, vice-president, secretary, and treasurer.

Thus, the Protestant congregations have much local autonomy in governing their own secular affairs. But this does not mean that they also have, or take upon themselves, local autonomy in constructing ritual, nor does it mean that *within* the congregation there is no hierarchical control of ritual.

[2] This does not overstate the situation as it existed in Chicago in the late 1960s, although parishes in other social contexts may differ greatly in their de facto autonomy and in the relationship between clergy and local laity. Moreover, even the high degree of corporationlike organization I found in Chicago does not itself make the ritual less meaningful for participants. On the contrary, the place of a Roman Catholic parish in a highly organized formal church structure may well enhance the meaning of ritual, for the appeal of mass ritual is closely linked to its portrayal of a stable and orderly cosmos. In a parish like St. Clement, this stability and order are displayed not only by the ritual but also by the formal organization of the church.

The clearest case of local autonomy in secular affairs and centralized control of ritual is that of St. James. The support institutions of ritual in the Missouri Synod Lutheran Church are in practice similar to those of the Roman Catholic church even though they are not regulated by the same clear set of formal rules and procedures. The Missouri Synod does not require the printing of a nihil obstat and imprimatur in publications which are considered officially acceptable, but its publishing houses have informally enforced doctrinal criteria for approving what they publish. The cohesiveness of the Missouri Synod is still such that most local congregations use only those forms of ritual published by the synod's own publishing houses (such as the Concordia Press of St. Louis). The congregation of St. James worships according to the form published in the hymnals and ritual supplements from official synodal sources. Acceptance by the sacred hierarchy is still so important a part of this synod's religious culture that consensual acceptance of centralized control of ritual is possible without elaborate laws, even though local congregations are fiscally and juridically autonomous bodies.

St. Paul United Church of Christ belongs to a liberal denomination and therefore has much local autonomy in ritual matters as well as in fiscal matters. However, within this congregation the pastor has "in matters of liturgy, the authority of the pope."[3] This authority does not extend to secular affairs. The committees responsible for financial matters, for example, meet as a body of peers, including the pastor, to debate issues as equals and resolve disputes by vote.

Thus, although the denominational context of St. Paul's ritual is "democratic" and gives local autonomy, the congregational structure of the support institutions of ritual is hierarchical. The formal and customary manner of constructing ritual gives "papal" authority to the pastor. It is his responsibility not only to initiate sacred action within the ritual but also to initiate changes and innovations in the order and content of ritual. The ordinary dominance and exclusive right of initiation of the pastor are limited by the scope of tradition as perceived consciously and unconsciously by his congregation. There is, however, no formal and conscious mechanism for disputing the authority of the pastor.

Therefore, three kinds of institutions for the support of ritual have grown up in St. Paul: technical, ordinary, and crisis. The tech-

[3] From the transcript of an interview with a Lincoln Park clergyman.

nical institutions are the groups of musicians and artists who provide culturally acceptable settings for ritual. The ordinary institutions are oblique, informal, and circuitous methods of keeping track of unconscious beliefs and values without directly probing them. The two principal "ordinary" institutions for constructing the mass ritual of St. Paul are the pastoral call and the congregation's grapevine. In the pastoral call, the pastor visits homes and expresses general interest in the well-being of his parishioners. The tone of the visit is informal, but if there are any misgivings on the part of the lay persons, they are communicated to the pastor, sometimes directly, sometimes deferentially and indirectly. The congregation's grapevine is the regular series of informal conversations which go on before and after committee meetings, and before and after and during the meetings of the congregation's various clubs. What is significant about these conversations is that they are rarely if ever the specified formal concern of the committee or club in question.

The crisis institutions are the coalitions and individual performances which regularly occur when the borders of unconscious beliefs and values are threatened or transgressed. They are institutions for maintaining the relation between the symbolic structure of mass ritual and the actual unconscious beliefs of the congregation—the "rump session," the public outcry, and the act of quitting the group. All these forms of behavior arise from the fact that disagreement over ritual is not normal. When asked what a parishioner might do if he disagreed with the pastor's sermon, one clergyman said, "Well, if he has enough guts, he can go to the pastor in private and tell him." The phrase "if he has enough guts" indicates that unusual energy and self-assertion are required to deviate from accepted norms.

Rump sessions are informal and private gatherings of the temporarily discontented which take place outside the formal and public forums of communication within the group. In these gatherings, like-minded persons get together and gather energy to formulate their private understandings for the public forum. Alternatively, they may perform as a "lobby" to get their position into group policy by means of oblique, indirect, and informal communications.

In the social psychology of the group, this use of the terms *public* and *private* must stand for "conscious" and "unconscious" group bonds: beliefs and attitudes. What is done "in public"—that is, according to the normal rules of the congregation's processes—expresses the conscious identity of the group. "Publicity" in this sense brings into the light of consciousness what was formerly unconscious.

The Protestant pastor who presides over mass ritual in these churches must construct at least some of his ritual out of the continuous and fragmentary information he gathers from informal and oblique sources. Thus the peculiarity of the institution of mass ritual includes the pastor's relationship to what are authentically his own unconscious beliefs and values. He cannot compose ritual out of these institutions, because, as a servant of the congregation, he must take into consideration those preferences of the group which are transmitted to him principally through informal sources. This is the reason why, in mass ritual, the preacher very rarely uses the first-person singular pronoun. The nonegoic quality of mass ritual thus extends even to the activity of the pastor, and what we have referred to as the "ego-based" utterances of the clergy in mass ritual are ego-based only in this qualified sense: that they articulate—bring to conscious performance—the least common denominator of the unconscious beliefs of the whole congregation.

It is the pastor's responsibility to perform for the congregation a peculiar psychic task: to delve into the unconscious of his congregation and choose out of it those things which the members' conscious egos are willing to accept as part of their total psychic structure. What is peculiar about this process is that no member of the congregation is obliged to do it for himself or herself. This activity of "self-examination" is precisely the *activity* which is absent from mass ritual and which therefore gives it its tone of passivity.

The support institutions of mass ritual have therefore those characteristics of an association based on unconscious bonds and unconscious rules. For example, it is only when the assumed consensus is violated that persons are moved to organize themselves into divergent factions, and these factions characteristically behave "emotionally"—that is, with the defensive anger characteristic of a person threatened with ego loss.

The occurrence of crisis in the conduct of mass ritual and the development of "privatized" groups within a congregation indicate that the cohesiveness of the group requires the suppression from conscious attention of real differences in beliefs. When these differences arise, the group "disintegrates": that is, a person or persons leave it, thus constituting a new group; or a dissenting group retreats

to a sphere of private or unofficial existence. This private and unofficial existence is indicated by absence from the Sunday morning
worship service.[4]

The fragility of the group cohesiveness and identity of a congregation practicing mass ritual indicates that the group is made up of
individuals who lack "psychic integrality." This means that what
these persons accept as "self" excludes motivations, desires, and
beliefs which are real but have been repressed. The possession of
psychic integrality, on the other hand, means that the conscious
ego stands open to a continuous stream of new discoveries about
its own motivations, desires, needs, and beliefs. The "I" in this
case is not threatened by others' different interpretations of common
symbols, because this integral "I" recognizes that its own interpretations of meanings are provisional. Their provisional character
arises from the fact that they are seen as arising from a psychic
sphere—within the "self"—that is both molded by idiosyncratic
experience and not fully exposed to the scrutiny of conscious
introspection. Whatever arises from other persons is treated with
the same ego-based review as whatever arises from one's own unconscious. It is questioned and tested for its correspondence with
the other perceptions of reality which make up integral psychic
activity.

At this point in the analysis, clinical and anthropological perspectives merge, for every culture is a symbol system which encompasses
a *limited* world view. There are always alternative systems. But the
psychic function of culture is to relieve the human actor from
continually expending energy on constructing an integral meaning
system. The oceanic experience of which religious mystics speak
may be perceived as "dangerous" on many counts, but one is that
it erodes the boundaries of the meaning system within which pragmatic action not only performs the technical tasks necessary for

---

[4] Two such groups were noteworthy in St. Paul. One was the group producing
an "experimental" Sunday worship service. This ritual was held at 9:00 A.M., a
very early hour for Protestants, in various rooms away from the central sanctuary. A conscious acceptance of the legitimate difference between the new
and traditional styles would have been symbolized by holding both rituals at
the same hour of the day.

The other group was the Christian Education Committee, most of whose
members rarely attend the worship service. They thus symbolize a latent change
in the congregation's identity which has not yet surfaced to group consciousness. As they develop a program of "study sessions with lay leaders," which
is in fact interaction ritual, they are, as one member pointed out, becoming
an "ersatz church."

physical survival but also is itself declared meaningful at a "spiritual" and moral level.

Thus, mass ritual is an expression of stable culture. This particular culture assigns the role of initiating change in the culture to ritual (religious specialists). To change this arrangement requires a change in the integral symbol system, and this transformation of a whole symbol system is a specific psychic task which in turn requires the support institutions characteristic of interaction ritual.

THE SUPPORT INSTITUTIONS OF INTERACTION RITUAL

Interaction ritual requires of its participants a high level of familiarity with one another's personal biographies, so that differences in individual interpretations of common symbols can be seen as coming from a common source: each person's effort to make the idiosyncrasies of his or her own personal biography meaningful through the meaning-giving power of religious symbols. A congregation performing interaction ritual develops institutions designed to foster this degree of familiarity. Thus, in the congregation of Three Crosses, for instance, there are a number of affect-oriented associations and meetings which do not directly support ritual but which sustain the kind of community that must exist to support interaction ritual. These affect-oriented associations are different from the issue-specific clubs that usually characterize parishes and congregations. They do not center on common activities or interests such as visiting the sick, caring for the church, or taking part in athletic activities. Nor are they limited to specific age or sex groups. Rather, they bring their members together on the basis of their diversity of interests, age, and sex.

In the Church of the Three Crosses, the principal form of such association is called a *Koinonia group*.[5] The members of the congregation divide themselves up according to the night of the week

[5] *Koinonia* is the Greek word for community. It is a word which occurs frequently in the Greek version of the New Testament, and it came into the vocabulary of contemporary Christianity through the enlivened interest in scholarly study of the Bible. Nowadays many lay persons know a number of Greek words, which they use to express their sense of wanting to fully understand the original meaning of the New Testament. *Koinonia*, *agape* (nonerotic, spiritual love), *logos* (word), and *pneuma* (spirit) are some of the Greek words whose use has increased recently.

when it is most convenient for them to get together. This procedure gives rise to three or four groups of ten to twelve persons who meet twice a month. The agendas of such meetings are very loose, and the discussions range over a wide field of religious, political, and cultural topics of interest to the members of the group. What holds the groups together is the members' interest in one another's personal biographies. It is important, they feel, to find out where people are coming from in their commitment to find meaning in the traditional symbol system of Christianity. Once people feel that they really know one another, the "K groups" fall into disuse, and mutual familiarity is sustained by other, more occasional meetings. These include a monthly theater party, in which the whole congregation goes to see a movie or play and then joins in a party and discussion at the home of one of the members; seasonal parties, such as before Christmas, or for the pastor's birthday, or on the occasion of someone's moving out of the community; and, twice a year, a weekend retreat in the country. This retreat is devoted to group discussions, eating together, playing volleyball, square-dancing, and a festival worship service.

These affect-oriented meetings develop a sense of diversity in the congregation. "Our diversity" is repeatedly mentioned in Sunday morning worship services—sometimes in formal prayers composed by a worship task force, but more usually in the obiter dicta of the pastor in his capacity of master of ceremonies for the ritual. I originally thought that this "diversity" was an element of false self-image, because the members of the congregation appeared to be more than ordinarily homogeneous in respect to social categories such as income, education, occupation, and place of residence. But the diversity referred to is that created by a heightened sense of individual differences in personal biography, and the intent of the ritual is to provide full expression of this diversity.

The common element which binds this diversity together is the willingness to revise one's personal biography, to accept one's own belief as idiosyncratic, to open oneself to criticism and self-criticism. This kind of community is closed only to those who are unwilling to expose their personal styles and actions and beliefs to the discussion and judgment of other members of the congregation.

When members of the congregation of the Church of the Three Crosses were asked why they belonged to this church rather than some other, two reasons were most frequently given. One was the "sense of freedom" they felt in the group, and the other was the feeling of "real sharing" in the church. The sense of freedom refers to the fact that common symbols are open to personal inter-pretation. The sharing refers to the fact that these interpretations are shared without being imposed. The congregation has had at least two regular members who refuse to call themselves Christians, "for reasons of their own." The majority shared the ritual with them but did not impose the use of the label "Christian."

The meetings of the executive council of the congregation are influenced by this policy of continually confronting the group and the members with the diversity of personal interpretations of reli-gious symbols. The executive council is formally "task-oriented"— that is, it must make decisions on the buying and selling of property, disbursement of income, use of the church's physical plant, and so on. But each meeting of this council begins with a discussion of some common reading, chosen for its ability to challenge present beliefs and opinions.[6] The reading is referred to as "worship and education." One pastor comments:

> In our early discussions, a big thing that came up was "we don't want to have church meetings." We want any meetings that this church has to be significant, meetings that are dealing with important things in our lives, and to keep to a minimum any structure which would force us to sit around and talk about unimportant things. This is basically what most meetings they went to were. Out of that came the suggestion that every meeting start with worship and education for the task of mission. Out of this came the conviction that we have to worship to-gether, and be accountable, and carry on education in order to think that every committee which has been significant in this church has done that, and those that haven't, have just withered away and died.

This style of personal interaction, generated in Koinonia groups and maintained even in the task-oriented meetings of the congrega-tion, is applied specifically to the task of constructing Sunday morning ritual in the groups called the worship task force. The task force is the institution that most directly supports the performance of ritual.

The worship task force meets regularly on any weekday evening that is convenient for all its members. The four to six members of the group change each month, according to a sign-up sheet or in response to the pastor's personal request that those who haven't

---

[6] In 1970 this committee read *The Church* (Philadelphia: Westminster Press, 1968), a theological discussion by Colin Williams, and in 1971 they were reading *The Technological Society* (New York: Random House, Vintage, 1967) by Jacques Ellul.

served recently join the month's group. There are months when not enough volunteers can be gathered, and so the pastor fills in. But the congregation does not go for more than three months without this kind of lay participation in the construction of ritual.

Before the task force meets, each member is given the series of scripture readings which are recommended for the following Sunday. In the meeting, each member gives his or her personal reactions to the scripture pericope. Discussion of the differences generated by these reactions goes on at some length, from one to three hours. Then follows a discussion of how to build a worship service around the sacred text accepted for the Sunday—which may be the recommended passage from the Bible, some other biblical passage, some secular reading, or a combination of these. Usually the ritual is built according to the sequence of segments: Preparation for the Word, Confrontation with the Word, Response to the Word, and the normal repertoire of operations; the actual composition of the ritual is left to individual members of the group. If anything has to be printed in the weekly bulletin, it is given to the congregation's secretary (by Friday) for typing and mimeographing. If the content of operations does not require typing, the group meets just before the worship service and arranges who is to say and do what during the ritual.

In giving the Sunday sermon, the pastor acts as spokesman for the worship task force. His sermon usually relates the issues which came up in the group's discussion of "the Word," explicitly beginning with a sentence such as: "The worship task force struggled over the meaning of this morning's Word and came up with the observation that. . . . " The members of the task force and of the congregation at large see this as an expression of his technical specialization in the handling of verbal symbols. He is a good (practiced) speaker, and so he gives the speech. Other members of the congregation compose other operations of the ritual, and so all share in the construction of the sacred symbol.

According to the members of the Church of the Three Crosses, the experience of participating in a worship task force is essential to the experience of the community which constitutes the congregation. The experience of the worship task force is itself religious and is thought of as worship. What happens on Sunday morning, then, is simply a more public dramatization of the meaning discovered in the smaller group and, furthermore, a dramatization of the process of discovering those meanings.

The shift in emphasis from the worship task force to the formal ritual is from the meanings being worked out in interpersonal discussion to the process of discovering emergent meanings, which is shared and participated in by all members of the group. In the "work group" the process is performed, and in the ritual the process is symbolized. The principal symbol in the ritual of this process is the practice of multiple and random initiation of utterance and action in the operations of the ritual. As one pastor commented:

> My understanding of the church's organization—though two years ago it was more solid than it is now at this point—is to have enough experience in a group of eight to ten people so that you know you are free and can live without excuses. You never really have to say it, but that's what you're doing. So that's where it partly takes place, and what you do on Sunday morning is verbalize what you have known with the rest of your life. In the smaller group, it's a requirement of the presence of others, although when you're actually doing it, it isn't adequate. And then the other thing is that it is the hope that you hold out, that someday you *will* be that free with each other.[7]

SUMMARY AND CONCLUSION

What emerges from our comparative data on four congregations in Lincoln Park is that a consistent set of differences—on the levels of exegesis, operational patterns, and spatial arrangements—distinguishes two kinds of ritual.

On the exegetical level, there is a difference between egoic and objective interpretations of ritual. According to the egoic interpretation, all those engaged in the performance of the ritual are—in that performance—equally in contact with the sacred. Therefore, the symbols and the symbol system expressed in ritual can also be produced in the ritual. The process by which symbols are produced as well as "manipulated" is the one alluded to in the phrase " . . . one, two, or five people saying what that scripture means to them." According to the objective interpretation, the sacred is an

---

[7] This verbatim quote allows us to look at cultural change as if we were seeing life emerge under a microscope. The disjointed and jerky language which yet enunciates innovative models of generating religious meanings presents the new emerging from the old in the course of everyday life. Too often we only see new institutions or ideas in their maturity. Here we have a chance to glimpse how tentatively they are aborning. The existence of this process—and its structure—is one of the main points of this work.

object "out there" ("up there"?) for all participants in the ritual, but to different degrees. On the one hand, there is a "Christ event," which "man has very little to do with"; on the other hand, there are some worshipers who have been "set apart," carefully prepared, whose responsibility it is to mediate between this objective sacred and the lay people. In this interpretation, both clergy and laity are outside the sacred, but the clergy are "closer to it" than lay people.

On the operational level, the same difference is expressed: between a ritual which objectifies the sacred and hierarchizes participants and a ritual which levels the hierarchy of participants and treats the sacred not as an object "out there" but as a zone of activity immediately accessible to all participants, and also complex in the sense that it is both objective and personal. It is objective in that it gives rise to objective statements (for example: "I think that this event means such and so"). It is personal in that it involves the whole person who makes such a statement (for example: "I don't know why, but I am deeply convinced that this is the way we should pray").

The separation between clerical and lay roles is frequently expressed in mass ritual by symbolic clothing and by the custom of assigning to the clergy the right to initiate sacred action and to the laity the role of receiver/listener in the ritual. Besides initiating sacred action in the ritual, clergy control the "flow of the liturgy." They do this as bearers of tradition, as experts, as the ordained. There is an inner logic of mass ritual by which the objectification of the sacred and its separateness from the profane world call for separations among believers, between those set apart and ordinary folk. The gulf between the sacred and the profane is also manifested in language. There are two languages for mass ritual: one sacred and one secular. Sacred language is formal and may use archaisms; it avoids colloquialisms and slang. Secular language—the language of everyday life, with its slang and colloquialisms—is excluded from this kind of ritual. In music, too, the repertoires of mass ritual draw the line at various places, but all exclude secular, popular, contemporary music. The processions of mass ritual are also hierarchical: lining up participants according to their degrees of sacred position.

In interaction ritual, anyone may initiate sacred action. The order of ritual is controlled by egalitarian groups of members of the congregation. The specialists in the group which performs interaction ritual are technical specialists, not sacred specialists. Their function is not to "manipulate symbols of the sacred" but to manipulate various technical classes of symbols (language, music, art) according to the meanings determined by a collective process of discussion, experiment, and criticism. The language of interaction ritual is the everyday language of the participants, including slang and colloquialisms. The sacred text of this ritual is not only the Bible but also any "secular" writing in which any participant finds meaning. Thus, all operational boundaries in interaction ritual become fluid. The "sacred" is somehow embedded in the "profane." Plastic bread wrappers draped over the arms of the cross in the Church of the Three Crosses symbolize the all-inclusiveness of this image of the sacred.[8] All of everyday experience contains it, points to it, and is rendered meaningful by it. The totally trivial is included in the ritual precisely to define the scope of the sacred as permeating all of human experience.

At the positional level, the same two images of the relationship between the sacred and the experience of everyday life are expressed. In mass ritual, the boundaries between the chancel and the rest of the sanctuary (in Roman Catholic churches, between the sanctuary and the nave) are clearly marked and behaviorally reinforced. Ordinary members of the congregation (lay persons) do not enter the area in which the sacred drama is performed. Even ordained persons put on distinctive clothes which symbolize a special identity in the ritual. In interaction ritual, the spatial arrangements are characterized by a permeable center of low salience, for interaction ritual still recognizes the sacred as a special sphere of experience. But the low salience of the center of the ritual space, the vague boundary between it and the rest of the ritual space, and the free traffic into and out of the center symbolize the ready access to the sacred which all participants are assumed to have.

The support institutions of mass ritual and interaction ritual maintain the same set of differences. Mass ritual is constructed by the more thoroughly socialized participants: clergy, theologians, and ritual experts. Their socialization makes them more attuned

---

[8] Some time in the fall of 1970, two plastic bread wrappers appeared, one draped over each arm of the cross. I do not remember how they got there or what comment accompanied their appearance. They stayed for several months until they got dirty. During their stay very little comment was made. But they were judged to be appropriate. My interpretation of this phenomenon is that it fits naturally with the assumptions of interaction ritual. The bread wrappers state the presence of the sacred *anywhere* in the profane world. They were there precisely because they were so *completely* mundane and trivial.

to the prescriptions of tradition and of official institutional authorities than to an institutionalized alliance of autonomous persons socialized in many different ways. Interaction ritual opens the process of constructing ritual so that anyone who wishes to construct sacred symbols with the group may do so. All persons who want to participate are assumed to have the fully authentic contact with the sacred out of which ritual is constructed. All such persons are considered to have valid contributions to make to the authorship of ritual. This "wanting to participate" must only include a respect for all others involved in the production of ritual. In the Church of the Three Crosses respect therefore encompasses the traditional symbols of Christianity. The God of the Bible and the death and resurrection of Jesus are presumed to be symbols of persons and events which command elemental respect.

CHAPTER 9

Transitional Processes

Mass ritual and interaction ritual differ in the ways in which they define and use the boundaries between the sacred cosmos and the profane world. They differ in the kinds of behavior they elicit from their participants in church, and possibly in secular spheres of life as well. Mass ritual elicits passivity in church and dependence on religious authorities in the public conduct of the religious aspect of church life. Interaction ritual elicits active participation in ritual, which amounts to directive control over the content, the structure, the very *order* of ritual process, and directive participation in all aspects of institutional religion.

The often inarticulate but always deeply felt preference of religious believers for one or the other of these two styles of ritual indicates that they represent different psychic styles whose roots are in the hidden strata of human motivation. It will be enlightening, therefore, to examine the actual process by which a group of persons change their ritual style—and presumably their psychic style—from that of mass ritual to interaction ritual.[1] I have gathered detailed information on such a process in the Church of the Three Crosses between June 1964 and July 1970, during which time a full transformation of

[1] There are also processes of transition from interaction ritual to mass ritual, or their functional equivalents. If interaction ritual is a symptom of a high degree of ego autonomy vis-à-vis authoritative institutions of society, then Max Weber would suggest that it is a very unstable social phenomenon, dependent on the occurence of "charisma." But all charisma, Weber seems to say, becomes subject to the process of "routinization." Thomas O'Dea has commented on this and other transitions from autonomy to submissiveness in "The Five Dilemmas in the Institutionalization of Religion," *Journal for the Scientific Study of Religion* 1 (October 1961): 32–39.

the ritual of this congregation took place. I have also gathered data on a similar process in St. Paul United Church of Christ, a process which was still incomplete in 1971 but which appears to be concerned with the same basic issue as in the Church of the Three Crosses: ego autonomy vis-à-vis authoritative institutions.

In both cases, we appear to be dealing with the cultivation of charisma, in that both processes appear to have been initiated by a charismatic individual, a minister. It need not be thus in every case, but the structural position of the clergy in organized religion makes their charisma most effective in such institutions. The charisma of lay persons must usually find expression outside the institutions of organized religion.

In Three Crosses, the process has one general characteristic which should be pointed out before going into details. It is the *piecemeal* nature of change. The history of religion is indeed characterized by fully formed breaks with religious or social tradition. The action of the great prophets and religious founders is integral from the begining. The prophet typically spends a significant period of time in meditation and contemplation away from the society which socialized him/her and returns "from the desert" with an ego-autonomous, charismatic, and integral message of change: "It is written . . . but I say. . . ."

But this classic confrontation between the prophet and institutional society is simply a dramatic form of a social process which can occur less obtrusively. Persons who are not free to retreat to the "desert" may still develop intimations of autonomy in the midst of society, by a process of experimentation, failure, revision, and progress in which enduring intuitions are elaborated in a piecemeal process. What is perhaps most interesting about my observations is that this piecemeal process appears to begin with the revision of the most conscious dimensions of meanings—exegetical meanings—and becomes complete with the revision of the most hidden dimensions of meaning—positional meanings.

"GETTING ON THE RIGHT SIDE"

One of the pastors of the Church of the Three Crosses said in 1970: "It took us over four years to get on the right side of this thing." By "this thing," he meant the disputes in the community of Lincoln Park over the implementation of urban renewal. By "the right side" he meant advocacy of a high percentage of low-income housing for the area.

While this process of "getting on the right side" in a local political dispute was going on, the process of change in the congregation's ritual style was also occurring. In January of 1964, the ritual of this congregation had the operational and positional characteristics of mass ritual.[2] There were clear differences between the role of clergy and the role of lay persons in the ritual as regards the initiation of sacred action and the choice of elements of ritual. The linguistic style of the ritual was formal and archaic. Most prayers were either exact quotations from traditional biblical sources or close paraphrases of biblical texts. The musical style drew from traditional virtuoso and popular religious sources, with exclusive use of the organ for musical accompaniment.

The only element of ritual which had begun to change at this time was the content of the sermons. The pastor in 1964 had already begun, in the words of one of his successors, "to bring the community into that congregation."

In July 1970 the last moving of furniture in the church's sanctuary took place, thus transforming the spatial arrangements of the worship space from a meeting hall with a stage to a worship space with a center of low salience. This moving of furniture marked the end of the transitional process for the group from mass ritual to interaction ritual.

The time between these two events—the sermons of "involvement" in early 1964 and the moving of furniture in 1970—was spent in gradual change of the style of the ritual. Two sets of events will serve as the basis for a schematic history of these changes. In the first set are changes in the social structure of the congregation and its environment. The second set is composed of changes in the manner of performing ritual in the congregation.

The thematic events in the social history of the congregation are as follows:

1. June 1964: The arrival of the two men who became co-pastors

[2] Since my research in the field began only in 1969, I was not able to procure all the "exoteric interpretations" of this ritual in 1965. I did have the memories of members of the congregation to draw on, as well as the complete file of programs for every Sunday ritual going back to 1955. The esoteric interpretations, however, were the same as the ones I commented upon in chapter 8. The official Protestant and Roman Catholic theologies of worship were were substantially the same in 1965 as in 1970.

of the congregation, and the series of congregation council meetings which followed their installation.

2. June 1965: One pastor and the other pastor's wife go to Selma, Alabama, to take part in the march there.

3. October 1966: The merger of the Second Evangelical United Brethren Church with St. James United Church of Christ to form the Church of the Three Crosses, and the congregational bylaws arising from that merger.

4. November 1966: The meetings of the first Koinonia groups in the newly merged congregation.

5. August 1968: The Democratic convention demonstrations in Lincoln Park.

6. October 1968: The beginning of regular participation in the composition of the worship service by a worship task force composed of lay members of the congregation.

7. June 1970: One of the co-pastors leaves for a new assignment.

The thematic events in the history of the congregation's worship service are as follows:

1. September 1964: The beginning of talkback as a regular part of the ritual.

2. June 1965: The change in the time of worship from 11:00 A.M. to 10:00 A.M.

3. July 4, 1965: The first use of a secular reading in the worship service.

4. June 12, 1966: The placing of the sermon immediately after the scripture reading in the worship service, instead of the separation of these two operations by a series of congregational and pastoral prayers which placed the sermon at the very end of the worship service.

5. July 31, 1966: The first use of the guitar in the worship service.

6. January 1967: The first singing of the hymn "The Lord of the Dance."

7. February 11, 1968: The Sunday when no biblical readings were used in the worship service but only readings from secular sources.

8. November 1969: The first use of the three-segment service labeled Preparation for the Word, Encounter with the Word, Response to the Word.

9. November 1969: The first stage of the furniture moving,

changing the focal point of the ritual space from in front of and above the congregation to the midst of it.

10. July 1970: Completion of the spatial rearrangements by moving the congregation's large cross from a position against the front wall of the old chancel to a freestanding position in the "center of law salience" in the middle of the sanctuary.

THE PASTORS' INITIATIVE

Since the two sets of events make up a single scenario, we shall comment on them in chronological order.

When the two new co-pastors of the Second Evangelical United Brethren Church took office, they came with a certain clear conviction about the structure of a religious congregation. One pastor reported:

> We wanted to use the council meeting, even the first one, for getting out some understandings and try to ground it in, you know, the word. And there was hot give and take, especially in the beginning, and not all of it was directed back and forth between lay people and us, but among those people back and forth. There was real, honest disagreement among them. And there were actually points when they were yelling, and very vocal disagreements; and then, afterwards, people had their arms around each other and were kind of joking and everything else. We were both amazed, I remember, after the first council meeting, that there was that kind of intensity of disagreement, and yet it seemed like afterwards, you know, it wasn't just a superficial putting your arms around each other; they seemed to live with each other. That was one of the first things.
>
> . . . We were coming out of the fifties to the high point of religious attendance and all that stuff [when we were in the seminary], and I think that on our part there was a certain rebellion against that . . . that's not really what the theology we believe in speaks about. . . . I would say that [what we believed in was] the servant concept and trying to make, uh, to create the matter of commitment as lying with the people as opposed to being just a social kind of thing, which the church of course is strong on. . . .

"The theology we believe in" had for one of the pastors, antecedents going as far back as boyhood experiences. He tells of his father's reasonable and nonauthoritarian religious belief and of his own shock when as a young boy he discovered that in his hometown there was a white section and a black section, and that it was not safe for a black person to be in the white section after dark. This warm relationship with a reasonable, religious father, on the one hand, and the discovery of institutional racism, on the other, led this pastor to question the inviolability of institutional authorities. At a young age, he was already developing notions of autonomy vis-à-vis the authoritative institutions of American society.

The two co-pastors went to the same seminary at the same time. One of them was the convener of a study group of seven seminarians who, over the course of their college and seminary years, banded together to train themselves in the theological grounds for attitudes and beliefs which were more "liberal" than those of the traditionalist and conservative institutions they attended. In their seminary days they read such literature as George Webber's account of an ecumenical ministry in East Harlem, New York, in the late 1950s.[3] Among the seminary faculty they received encouragement from a few liberal professors (one of whom was fired in 1968), but on the whole they sustained themselves as a dissenting group within the structure of their church.

After ordination, the two co-pastors went to different assignments. Two years later they heard of a vacancy in the inner city of Chicago, and between them persuaded church officials and the congregation of Second EUB to accept them as a team: two men with equal rank as co-pastors. This nonhierarchical arrangement was a novelty to both the denomination and the congregation, but the two young clergymen prevailed.

Both pastors brought with them to their new congregation some definite views on what the structure of such a group ought to be, plus some very unclear images of the process that would lead to such structures. Their images of religious faith and of community launched a process of controversy which found its first expression in the congregation council meetings described above, attended by approximately twenty of the most active members of the congregation.

The first stormy meetings of the new co-pastors with the members of their congregation began the dialectic of confrontation between

[3] During their seminary years the pastors also read the liberal and innovative works of Dietrich Bonnhoeffer and the classical writers of modern Protestantism, such as Karl Barth, Paul Tillich, and Rudolf Bultmann. The case of Barth is interesting because more conservative pastors have found a conservative theology in this writer, whereas the young pastors have found a more existential and liberal theology. This suggests that the operative theology of the ministerial candidates had been formed before their formal study. Two factors seem most important for the formation of this operative theology: the manner in which religious authority was imposed in the home, and the pastor's confidence in the legitimacy of powerful secular institutions. This second factor seems to hinge on the pastor's experience of racial discrimination. Personal contact with institutional racism seems to be the most potent single source of the delegitimization of institutionalized authority in his experience.

different psychic styles in that group of believers. The dynamics of these meetings—with "hot give and take" during them and then people putting "their arms around each other" afterward—symbolizes the pattern of struggle characteristic of this kind of conflict. On the one hand, it is true that some members of the congregation were, in 1964, just waiting to see in which direction the new pastors were going to go, and left the congregation when it became clear that the direction started by the previous pastor in his "sermons on involvement" was to be continued. On the other hand, it is also true that many people who had worshiped in the style of mass ritual for their whole previous lives stayed in the congregation and went through a process of change which was very demanding. The fundamental process was the bringing of latent disagreements to the conscious level—"vocal disagreements," with a "lot of yelling"—without permitting them to become the basis for group fission. The minimal psychic equipment for this process was the ability to say, "I may be wrong," and to undertake the revision of personal world view consequent upon such a statement.

The initial meetings, therefore, defined the situation for the congregation. Those who eventually left began to leave at this time, and those who stayed decided to do so at this time.

THE INSTITUTION OF THE TALKBACK

After these initial meetings, the pastors continued to bring the demand for involvement and autonomy into the ritual process. Their first step was twofold: they continue the "sermons of involvement" of their predecessor, and they instituted talkback as a regular part of Sunday morning activities, immediately following the formal liturgy.

The talkback became the principal means for the informal involvement of lay members of the congregation in the construction of ritual. Although it took four years for this informal involvement to take shape in a formal lay committee called the worship task force, the exchanges between pastors and congregation in the talkback served as an interim means of bringing lay members into the content and structure of the Sunday morning ritual.

The process which occurred depended on the pastors' listening respectfully to the judgments of the lay members about the suitability of sermons and other ritual operations and considering these judgments as valid as their own. The lay members of the congregation saw their own ideas expressed in the Sunday morning worship service and thus were gradually prepared for taking upon themselves the structurally autonomous responsibility of constructing a worship service. That it took four years for the worship task force to evolve suggests the potency of the habit of trained passivity in relation to authoritative definitions of the sacred cosmos (and therefore of any integral cosmology).

As was mentioned above, the talkback did not always function as an active part of the dynamics of ritual. It frequently lapsed into a period of informal conversations among small groups of persons. But its very existence on a regular basis made it available when feedback was necessary. Thus the members of the congregation knew that, when they wanted to do so, they had a legitimate vehicle for confronting the whole congregation with purely personal perceptions, which were felt to be authentic and legitimate. The regularity and permanence of the institution were a potent symbol of the normative commitment of the group to recognizing and declaring legitimate a need which is "occasional"—that is, which occurs as a random rather than a routine event.

Although the talkback provided a regular mechanism for autonomous expression of personal beliefs, the sermons in the first years of the pastors' tenure were also critically important in the transitional process from mass ritual to interaction ritual.

> At first the ritual's form was pretty well set up by tradition and had to be used, plus any creativity we could put into it. Having two ministers was helpful. . . . Basically we used people who had some gifts. *Yeah, we intentionally used that morning worship service as that kind of education.* And if you go back and look at the bulletin, I'm sure, I think the first summer when we were here, or at least in the fall, we had a whole series on the church, the church's position, the church as a forgiveness, the church as . . . I don't know if it was pioneer or revolutionary or something, but there were five or six Sundays we just went along, you know, saying this understanding of the church.

These sermons, we should note, were not a change in the structure of the ritual but only in the content of one operation of the ritual. The sermon is the operation of ritual most subject to the control of the minister. Tradition gives him some freedom in what he shall say. But tradition was still in control of this ritual, and although the message was one of "commitment as lying with the people," the operational and positional meaning of the ritual as still hierarchical at this stage, prescribing the passive and mass participation of the lay members of the congregation.

FIRST CHANGES IN OPERATIONAL STYLE

The first operational break with the authority of tradition occurred almost a year after the new pastors came, when the whole congregation was called upon to agree to change the hour of morning worship. The basic issue was not the time at which to meet but the right of the congregation to dispute the authority of tradition. The authority of tradition is one element of institutionalized authority—the socialized aspects of self which are different from the purely subjective self and which prescribe behavior for the total self.[4] By changing the time of worship, the congregation began the process of declaring itself independent of the whole class of behavior-specifying social institutions, of which tradition is only one example. Independence in this case does not mean rebellion from or contempt for such institutions. They may still be treated with respect, but they are also treated as "mere equals."

Also during the summer of 1965, as noted, the operation called the secular reading began to be used. Because such an operation requires one to perceive the sacred nature of a writing which is not approved by tradition, even listening to it requires an ego-based judgment by the believer.

During the previous year, the pastors had begun to change another aspect of the ritual structure—namely, the labels describing the segments of the ritual. The four segments of the ritual had been called Quiet Preparation, Praise and Thanks, Confession and Petition, and Preparation for Christian Living. During 1965, these labels began to change with great frequency. Almost every week, an altered form would appear.

The changes of labels called for less active participation by the congregation than the secular readings. Such labels, as pointed out, are exegetical in character. They are a theological commentary on

---

[4] Peter Berger has considered the relationship between the "socialized self" and the "total self" in *The Sacred Canopy* (Garden City, N.Y.: Doubleday, 1967), pp. 54–56, 82–85. The part of his perspective which is relevant here is that he sees religion both as a part of and as a reinforcer of the laws and institutions of society as a whole. These laws and institutions are a class of phenomena perceived by the ego as powers *outside self* which define reality and prescribe behavior. The institutionalized definition of the sacred in mass ritual, therefore, is consistent with institutionalized definitions of secular reality. If, as our analysis suggests, interaction ritual betokens a change in the source of definitions of *sacred* reality, from institutions to the members of a face-to-face group, we must still ask what, if any, are the forms of asserting autonomy vis-à-vis secular—that is, social, economic, political, and cultural—definitions of reality.

the meaning of the ritual, and since theology is traditionally the specialty of the clergy, the pastors could change them without departing markedly from their traditional roles and without actively involving the lay members of the congregation. But a reading from a secular source calls for participation of the congregation in a radically new mode of perception.

The action of worship is perceived by the religious believer as contact with and response to "the sacred." It is a major shift in the perceptual style of getting in touch with the sacred when the secular reading is placed immediately next to a reading from a traditionally sacred text in the context of formal ritual; for the secular reading is perceived as coming from the profane segment of the world. In principle, the inclusion of the secular in ritual demands that the believer be ready to perceive the sacred *anywhere,* not just in the traditional and culturally prescribed loci such as temples, sacred texts, and ordained clergy.

Still, in 1965 the pastors themselves chose the secular readings, and they commented on them in sermons. Although the mode of perceiving the sacred was markedly changed for the whole congregation by the introduction of secular readings, the lay members were still not called upon formally to specify where in all the world they perceived the sacred or to initiate expression of their perceptions in the formal ritual.

During this time, the congregation became aware that its musical style also was to be questioned:

> [The music we have reflects] a different age, a different understanding. It does not reflect who we are at this point. This music certainly does not reflect any of the urban images . . . very rural-oriented and all that. I think there's one hymn in there, "Praise to Thee, O God, for Cities." It was written in 1956 by a guy who went to the same seminary we did. So we taught them that.

The critical element of this comment is the reference to time. The traditional music was "of a different age" and did not reflect "who we are at this point." This is concern for maintaining the autonomous ego at the center of world-maintenance processes. Changes in technology and social organization change the loci of power in society and therefore the loci of good and evil for the religious believer. If the believer is to judge contemporary institutions and persons against a set of ultimate values and an integral view of the cosmos, his ritual must review contemporary issues and institutions. The music of all cultures—including the contemporary and popular music of America—

has always been able to express issues for value judgment with an emotional power not contained in spoken or written words.

REARRANGING THE ORDER OF OPERATIONS

From the time the new pastors arrived until the summer of 1966—two years later—the order of operations and segments of the ritual was unchanged. During the summer of 1966, however, the pastors began to rearrange the order of operations. Previously, the sermon had been at the end of the worship service, separated from the other climax of the word-oriented ritual—the scripture reading—by five operations.[5] The sermon's position at the end of the ritual—followed only by the closing operations of blessing, final hymn, and organ postlude—was a manifestation of the increased importance of the minister in Protestant churches since the Reformation. By its place at the end of the ritual, the sermon "competed with" the scripture reading for importance. In the course of the worship service, the sacred Word came in the middle and was read with appropriate solemnity, but the structure of the ritual made the sermon the operation one was to look forward to. When the sermon was done, *then* the ritual was complete and everybody could go home.

This symbolic expression of the importance of the pastor in the local congregation indicates the influence of secular institutions on religious symbolism. For the egalitarianism of the doctrine of the priesthood of all believers could hardly continue to flourish in a society becoming more centralized in every phase of life and more dependent on the advice of "experts." The fact that the ritual position of the sermon (that is, the "spoken Word") is in this case in conflict with the official theologies of Protestant belief is just another example of difference between the image of social order presented in a society's myths and the realities of the operational social order. The official theology is in this case the myth; the structure of the ritual expresses the operational social reality.

But in July of 1966, the pastors dropped the five operations between the scripture reading and the sermon and placed the operation

[5] The five operations were called Prayer Hymn, Silent Prayer, Pastoral Prayer, Congregational Prayer Response, and Lord's Prayer. They are all formal statements, in unison or by the minister alone, predetermined by a traditional manual, expressing the passive-dependent relationship of the congregation to the scripture reading, the interpretation to follow in the sermon, and the deity, who is the source of both operations.

of "offering" after the sermon.[6] This change put the scripture and the sermon (and the secular reading) in the middle of the temporal sequence of the ritual. The implications of this change are a reduction in the importance of the official clergy's commentary on the scripture and the blending of the secular word, scripture reading, and sermon into a unit which reduces the intensity of the boundary between the sacred and the profane. This change also provided a basis for upgrading the importance of the segment of ritual which would eventually be called Response to the Word. This specifically group-based interpretation of the implementation of the Word would hereafter consume a larger proportion of the time of worship as the congregation grew more confident in making spontaneous contributions to that segment of ritual.

Shortly after this change in the order of operation of the worship service, the guitar was introduced into the ritual. The use of the guitar also meant increased participation by the lay members of the congregation in choosing the songs to be sung in worship.

CONTENT OF NEW BYLAWS

During the same summer of 1966, the congregation of the Second EUB Church was discussing the terms of its merger with St. James United Church of Christ. Out of those discussions came a new set of bylaws for the merged congregation of the Church of the Three Crosses. In these bylaws, the juridical position of the pastors was changed from co-heads of the congregation to members of the staff

[6] St. Paul United Church of Christ made a similar change in its order of worship two years later. This change occurred in November 1968, during Advent, which is the first part of the liturgical year in all Christian churches. In my interviews at St. Paul, I feel sure I did not get the whole story on this change. On the one hand, a reason given for the change was: "The Word needs to be read to the people, and then there is an opportunity immediately, *before the people have forgotten what they heard,* to open it up. And this is why we moved the Word and the sermon together." On the other hand, there was a report that this change was made at a meeting with some younger members of the congregation, who, I am sure, were not worried about forgetting the scripture before they heard the sermon.

I think what happened here is that the meaning of the separation of Word from sermon was an *operational* meaning, therefore "latent and partly hidden," in Turner's words. Thus, the reasons for changing it were also latent and partly hidden. The order of service was changed for the same reason as in the Church of the Three Crosses: a latent discomfort on the part of a liberal pastor and younger members of his congregation with the exaggerated emphasis the old order placed on clerical authority.

of the congregation. The official expression of this change is in terms of voting power. The new bylaws state:

> The EPC[7] shall be composed of seven laymen and the lay leaders of this congregation . . . and the following non-voting members: the staff of this congregation and participating organizations. . . .

One of the co-pastors commented:

> There certainly is more of a sense of community. I think that really one of the key decisions which brought that about is . . . in the Old EUB Church, the minister was the head. He was the chairman of the Council. That's the way it still is in the United Methodist Church. And when we brought the two churches together, we even ruled ourselves out of voting power. . . . The pastors are seen simply as staff, which is a different concept, a different understanding of the discipline at this point.

By the time these new bylaws were written, therefore—in the summer of 1966, two years after the new pastors had taken office—the pastors' new understandings of the structure of a religious congregation had ceased to be their personal attitudes alone and had become shared by the members of the congregation to the extent that they were willing to pass bylaws excluding the pastors from voting power.

The changing place of the ministers in the congregation, as well as changes in the saliency of the traditions prescribing that the pastor must be head of the congregation, had already become symbolically expressed in the Sunday morning worship service. It is highly unlikely, in fact, that the members of the congregation would have had the self-confidence to assume this leaderless responsibility for themselves without the previous experiences of breaking with tradition over the hour of worship, rethinking the labels of the segments of the ritual, the exposure to secular readings from many contemporary sources, and the rearrangement of the relationship between the sermon and the sacred and secular readings. Even though this congregation would not have a formal worship task force in operation for another two years, the lay members of the group had already begun to take part in the construction of the ritual in many informal ways, principally through their participation in the talkback.

---

[7] EPC stands for Ecumenical Planning Council. At the time of the merger, the two congregations hoped for further mergers with other local churches. They even hoped to make the new congregation a kind of community organization, a broadly ecumenical forum for the whole neighborhood. This is why they called their church council by this name and why they refer to "participating organizations" in the bylaws.

When asked who initiated the proposal for making the co-pastors nonvoting members of the Ecumenical Planning Council, the pastors said that it came from the congregation. The lay members of the congregation report that the proposal came "naturally out of the group." This measure of consensus had developed as to the non-hierarchical structure of the group.

THE KOINONIA GROUPS

The merger of the two congregations also gave rise to the institution of Koinonia groups.[8] In order to build up personal relationships among the members of the two congregations—most of whom did not know one another well—the members of the new congregation agreed to meet in groups of no more than twelve, composed of members of both congregations. The meetings had a threefold effect on the new congregation. They contributed toward the relativizing of dogma, the legitimation of charisma, and the definition of the limits of community of which this congregation was capable.

In the words of the participants, the purpose of the Koinonia groups was for members "to get to know one another" and to do this by having "one, two, or five people [say] what that scripture means to them." This process of bringing to the surface the latent belief systems of the individual members of the group achieves the first two effects at the same time. It relativizes dogma by saying that dogmas stand for the cultural, social, familial, and personal biography of each individual. The prayers one prefers, the creeds one states, the hymns one feels affection for—these are artifacts of one's personal biography. Moreover, in the complex society in which the participants grew up, the variety of personal biographies is such that prayers and creeds and hymns take on a variety of meanings that cannot be reduced to acceptable *traditional* formulas. Since tradition probably derives much of its authority from the experience of childhood, and since the childhood of these persons has such variety—geographic, social, cultural, and religious as well as personal—common feelings based on that period of life cannot support any but the most general symbols —such as the cross, calling oneself Christian,[9] accepting the biogra-

[8] The only data I have on these first Koinonia groups are the accounts given by participants in interviews which took place five years later, in 1970. I did, however, take part in the Koinonia groups which met during 1970.

[9] There were even a few exceptions to this general symbol. As noted previ-

phy of Jesus as being of fundamental importance. Creeds and prayers and hymns have much more specificity than such general symbols.

Therefore, since the group does not have a full set of traditional religious-cultural artifacts to symbolize its solidarity, it must reach for another base, such as a collective acceptance of a single form of authority—which, in this case, sociologists refer to as *charisma*. By discussing their personal biographies and the belief systems that have resulted from those biographies, the members of the Koinonia groups were faced with the need to accept persons whose verbal definitions of faith and personal life styles were different from their own. This sensitivity to the relevance of personal charisma and its consequent legitimation as a basis for group affiliation were dramatized in my experience in many ways. For example, in an interview with an older couple in this congregation, I said: "Well, I am a graduate student and a bachelor, and I am not a celibate. That is, I fornicate. I guess you would know this anyway, but I'd like to know whether that makes a difference to you." The answers from the woman and the man were different. The woman said, "Well, Mike, I know you, and so I know that you would not hurt anyone in those kinds of relationships but would deal with them as honestly as possible." The man said, "Well, I guess I regard you as a little bit young. That's the stage of life you're in, and you will grow out of it."

My experience in the field supports the assertion that response was not a random event and that the key phase in the reply was, "Well, . . . I know you."

This kind of interaction turns the issue of religious belonging from criteria of creedal utterances and ethical styles to personal, charismatic qualities of the members. In order for this basis of group solidarity to exist, the members of the group must cultivate a degree of personal intimacy that permits the perception of those qualities.

The Koinonia groups also had the interesting effect of defining the limits of community solidarity for this congregation. On two occasions—in 1966 and again in 1970—members of Koinonia groups discussed Elizabeth O'Connor's book *Call to Commitment*,[10] an ac-

---

ously, at least one member of the congregation refused to refer to himself as a Christian, and the husband of another member would not join the congregation for the same reason. The members of the congregation saw the latter decision as whimsical, because it was evident to them that whether the man called himself a Christian or not, he believed all the important things they believed.

[10] New York: Harper and Row, 1963. The same author has written a second book on the experience of the Church of the Saviour entitled *Journey Inward, Journey Outward* (New York: Harper and Row, 1968).

count of the founding and development of the Church of the Saviour in Washington, D.C. This church, formed by a chaplain and other veterans of World War II, brought together a group of persons who expressed their religious beliefs not only in a set of common symbols and activities but also in an economically based communal group which shared incomes. The book provided a definition of the limits of community for the congregation of the Church of the Three Crosses. On both occasions, members of Koinonia groups raised the issue of "commitment" in the whole congregation, and the whole congregation agreed that economic communalism—the sharing of income and living space—was not something they could do.

Cultivation of personal solidarity in the Koinonia groups created pressure for economic expression of that solidarity. But the potency of the congregation's investment in economic individualism and competition proved to be too great an obstacle. Although the members trusted one another to take religious symbols seriously and to work toward developing a continuously revised set of symbols, they did not trust themselves or one another to live together as an extended family, pooling the economic resources of every individual and nuclear family in the congregation.

CHANGES IN SPECIFIC OPERATIONS

In the series of piecemeal changes which accumulated to transform mass ritual into interaction ritual, the process of experimentation of course continued through the year 1967. We have recorded only one experiment of that year whose success made it a permanent part of the congregation's ritual style. This was the discovery of the song "The Lord of the Dance," sung to the tune of a traditional Shaker hymn entitled "Simple Gifts."* The words of the hymn as used in the Church of the Three Crosses are as follows:

> I danced in the morning when the world was begun,
> And I danced in the moon and the stars and the sun;
> I came down from heaven and I danced on earth,
> At Bethlehem I had my birth.
>
> *(Chorus)*
>   Dance then, wherever you may be,
>   I am the Lord of the dance, said he,

> And I'll lead you all wherever you may be,
> And I'll lead you all in the dance, said he.
>
> I danced for the scribe and the pharisee,
> But they would not dance and they would not follow me;
> I danced for the fisherman, for James and John,
> They came with me and the dance went on. *(Chorus)*
>
> I danced on the Sabbath and I cured the lame,
> The holy people said it was a shame;
> They whipped and they stripped and they hung me high,
> And they left me there on a cross to die. *(Chorus)*
>
> I danced on a Friday when the sky turned black,
> It's hard to dance with the devil on your back;
> They buried my body and they thought I'd gone,
> But I am the dance and I still go on. *(Chorus)*
>
> They cut me down and I leap up high,
> I am the life that'll never, never die;
> I'll live in you if you'll live in me,
> I am the Lord of the dance, said he. *(Chorus)*

Without attempting an extended commentary on the multiple meanings of this song, I must observe that it is a remarkable example of the confluence of diverse social and cultural patterns which characterizes interaction ritual open to the full range of contemporary experience. This song—from an eighteenth-century American sect, with the addition of the sensuous, counter-Puritan imagery of the dance, with the recitation of the basic scenario of the New Testament, set in the context of a rational rather than an enthusiastic middle-class church—typifies the inclusive style of interaction ritual.

The centrality of the song in the musical style of this congregation is highly suggestive. One of its aspects is that although the congregation frequently *sings* the song, they do not actually *dance* to it. Vestigial dancing occurs, in hand clapping, foot tapping, and rhythmic body motions, but there is no full breaking into dance. This also may be interpreted as a strain between the ideal image of community fostered by ritual and the inherited inhibitions of traditional culture.

The song has become, in the words of the congregation, "one of our new traditions," and is sung during Sunday worship about once every three weeks. If they can't find a song that exactly fits the content of a specific ritual, they put in "The Lord of the Dance," because it fits almost anywhere.

The secular reading was in continuous use in the worship service of the Church of the Three Crosses from the summer of 1965, except for those occasions when the congregation worshiped with the more conservative Spanish-speaking congregation. This operation was always joined to the traditional reading from the Bible, except for one occasion early in 1968. On that Sunday, February 11, no scripture reading was used.[11] The "sacred texts" used were all "secular" readings, from the works of D. H. Lawrence, Leonard Cohen, Robert Frost, T. S. Eliot, and Piri Thomas, plus an excerpt from *Newsweek* magazine and a short film.

The importance of this event is that it exemplifies the kind of risk taking accepted by the members of the congregation in seeking new symbolic syntheses. Informants tell of the deliberateness with which that ritual was constructed and of their sense of having overstepped the bounds of authentic religious symbols without, at the same time, being embarrassed by their action. Even in 1970, the members of the congregation remembered that Sunday, not spontaneously but when I asked them about it because I was puzzled by the absence of scripture I had discovered while examining old Sunday bulletins. "Oh yes, they really worked on that." The positive nature of the reminiscences of that event, its salience in memory, and the fact that it was never repeated indicates the ego-autonomous openness of a group with a well-integrated commitment to the meaning-bearing capacity of their traditional symbols. The boundaries between meaning and nonmeaning are fluid, to be played with in a serious experimental style, in which mistakes are the desirable indicators of the true limits of their meaning system.

THE EFFECT OF THE 1968 CONVENTION DEMONSTRATIONS

The series of demonstrations which occurred at the Democratic National Convention in August 1968 and the role of the Church of the Three Crosses in those demonstrations reemphasized the commitment of the majority of the congregation to novel expressions of

[11] When I tried to find out when the worship task force began, the pastor and members of the congregation had a hard time remembering the exact date. They finally decided that it was in the fall of 1968, and the earliest group whose names they could recall constructed the ritual in October 1968. But when the service without scripture was mentioned, they recalled that a worship task force did compose that one, and they remembered at least one of the names of the lay persons involved in it. From this, I have concluded that worship task forces emerged sporadically and performed occasionally before they became a regular occurrence in the fall of 1968. This corresponds to the piecemeal experimental and tentative nature of the process of psychic growth (or simply change) which is implied by the transformation of mass ritual into interaction ritual.

political as well as religious beliefs and proved to be the "last straw" for some members of the congregation who were divided between their loyalties to the church of their earlier years and their commitment to the style of religious affiliation expressed in mass ritual.

The major involvement of the Church of the Three Crosses was limited to the demonstrations of Tuesday night in Lincoln Park. When, in the course of that day and evening, it became clear to some ministers of the North Side Cooperative Ministry who were patrolling the park that a large-scale confrontation between the police and the demonstrators was going to occur, they called all the members of NSCM and assembled a group of about fifty clergy and lay persons in the Church of the Three Crosses. Their meeting began at about 7:30 P.M. in an atmosphere of great tension. The group decided to go as a body into the park to try to mediate the conflict. The pastors of the Church of the Three Crosses agreed to the request of the group to take with them to the park the huge cross which at that time was located in the sanctuary of the church. This cross had previously been in St. James United Church of Christ, and, since the building of St. James was no longer used for worship by the merged congregation, it was the symbol of that congregation's existence. The ministers say they took the cross to the park both because it would enable them to be seen among the crowd and because the cross is a very diffuse symbol of their religious commitments.

After protracted attempts to negotiate with the police during the evening, the ministers found that the confrontation would in fact take place, since the demonstrators would not leave the park and the city officials would not suspend the 11:00 P.M. curfew ordinance. As the police lines formed to move on the demonstrators, the ministers with the cross were between the two groups. In the melee which followed, the cross fell to the ground, and the ministers were dispersed along with the demonstrators. When they went back to the park early the next morning to retrieve the cross, it was nowhere to be found.

Four members of the Church of the Three Crosses stopped attending church there because of this incident. They were all former members of St. James United Church of Christ. It was not only that the cross—the sole surviving symbol of their former church in the community—was lost, but also that, in their view, it had been "desecrated" by having been taken in among the "hippies."

But, for the majority of the congregation, the loss of the cross was a misfortune incurred in a worthy cause: the attempt to mollify a

violent confrontation. They saw its presence in the turmoil of political demonstration as symbolically correct. The intrusion of a sacred
symbol into a secular arena was but a continuation of the relation
between the secular and the sacred symbolized by their ritual every
Sunday. And the decision of the ministers and lay persons to bring
the cross into the park was seen as a proper exercise of their autonomous contact with the sacred. Although in retrospect it might be
criticized, it still partook of the risk taking which had by this time
become thematic in their ritual style.

After the old St. James cross was lost, the congregation began to
consider what kind of cross they should get to replace it. In a series
of formal and informal discussions, they decided to make one out
of the rubble of some building being torn down by the Department
of Urban Renewal. Later that fall—in October 1968—one pastor and
two lay members of the congregation were working in the church on
a Saturday afternoon and decided to get a new cross. They went to a
building being demolished on Larrabee Street and pulled a couple of
two-by-fours from the wreckage. One of the timbers was about fourteen feet long and the other about eight feet. Both were splintered
and worn and had many rusty nails still in them. The three men put
them together without alteration and placed the resulting cross in
the sanctuary of the church.

When the congregation assembled for worship the following day,
the new cross was there. The congregation responded with approval.
Although no formal mandate had been given, a decision had been
made "in our family style," and the implementation had been carried out as opportunity presented itself.[12]

THE WORSHIP TASK FORCE

It was at this time also that the worship task force became a regular
institution of the congregation of this church. Although there were
months, most often in the summer, when there were not enough
volunteers to make up a worship task force, the customary process of
composing a Sunday worship service was that it be done during the

[12] After the convention, too, the openness of the theological-ritual stance—
more than its proximity to the park—made it the site of some of the first organizing meetings of the Young Patriots, a politicized youth group of Appalachian
whites whose home turf was the Uptown area of Chicago, about two and a half
miles north of the Church of the Three Crosses. Some of these meetings were recorded on film and seen in the movie *American Revolution II*.

week for the following Sunday by a group of four or five lay persons meeting with one of the pastors. I took part in several of these worship task force meetings and found that the role of the pastor was not directive but only consultative. Furthermore, the meetings of the task force were themselves considered to be religious experiences. The process of a small group of persons meeting together to say what scripture did or did not mean to them was held to be of central importance in sustaining the life of the congregation.

Each member's input into the meetings was taken so seriously that anyone could exercise a veto on the content of the service. Consensus had to be achieved. If this was impossible, then each would make his or her contribution to the ritual by composing one or more operations. Then, in his Sunday sermon, the pastor would raise the points of difference for the whole congregation.

The worship task force grew out of the talkbacks which had been part of the congregation's Sunday morning activities for more than four years. The personal differences revealed in those talkbacks had for some time been taken into consideration by the pastors when they composed the ritual. The worship task force was more specifically task-oriented than the talkbacks. Besides the logistics of attending another evening meeting, the specificity of taking direct responsibility for the order and content of worship was the reason for the time gap between the beginning of the talkbacks and the regular practice of using a worship task force to compose the ritual.

The successful institution of a regular worship task force completed the change of the exegetical and operational meanings of the worship service to those of interaction ritual. But in the fall of 1968, the positional meaning of the worship service was still that of mass ritual. The chancel was still separated from the rest of the sanctuary by a railing at the edge of a raised platform. The ministers still presided from special chairs in the chancel, and the altar and the cross were placed in that more sacred area.

CHANGES IN POSITIONAL MEANING

During the early months of 1969, conversations during talkbacks and on informal occasions would sometimes turn to the arrangement of furniture in the sanctuary. Some older and more conservative members of the congregation resisted rearrangement of the furniture on such grounds as "it would make the church look like a theater."

But as the discussions continued, it became clear that the vast majority of the congregation found the old arrangement of furniture inappropriate and wanted something that would "bring us closer together" in the setting of ritual.

When the furniture was rearranged one evening by a group of persons who were at the church for another purpose, the issues had been discussed for such a long time that everybody knew the change was coming. Most members of the congregation greeted it with approval and relief. The few who disagreed decided to go along with the wishes of the majority, only expressing their disapproval by refusing to sit in the pews in the front, which now faced one another across the permeable center of low salience. These disagreements were known to all members of the congregation and were acknowledged in conversations by good-natured banter, teasing, and remonstrating.

It happened that at the same time the furniture was rearranged, the three-segment structure of the worship service also achieved stability, both in the number of segments and in their labels: Preparation for the Word, Encounter with the Word, Response to the Word.

When the general arrangement of the ritual space had been changed in late 1969, the cross had been left in its traditional place in the chancel against the far wall. Only as the implications of the change for the meaning of the empty chancel became clear did the inappropriateness of this location for the cross become manifest. The chancel was now empty and out of the line of positional focus of the ritual. The young children of the congregation would wander into the chancel during the service and play there. Thus, in July of 1970, the cross was moved to a position in the permeable center of low salience, where its size became much more noticeable and it literally loomed over the congregation gathered around it.

THE DEPARTURE OF A CO-PASTOR

During the summer of 1970, one of the co-pastors who had come in 1964 left to take the position of Youth Minister with an ecumenical ministry in another state. This was discussed at some length by the pastors and the congregation. The departing pastor's view was that his "job was done" at the Church of the Three Crosses. And although there was temporary anxiety in some segments of the congregation at losing one of the persons who had provided leadership during the years of change, the congregation members agreed that they could continue in the same direction without him and would consider it part of their own "outreach" to see him go to a new ministry, there to take part in transitions similar to the ones they had just experienced.

By this time, too, the battle over urban renewal in the Lincoln Park community area was, in the main, finished. The last stand of the Concerned Citizens Survival Front had taken place in February. The two main organizers of the Concerned Citizens were on the point of leaving the community, and its office on Lincoln Avenue fell into disuse by the fall. Members of the Church of the Three Crosses continued to be active in programs for developing small sites for low-income housing, but in the main, the congregation settled into the problems of creating programs for the new Lincoln Park, which they knew now was going to be populated largely by young, mobile, affluent single people and couples with one to two children.

LAUNCHING A NEW WORSHIP SERVICE

A new worship service was launched in St. Paul United Church of Christ on May 3, 1970, and was discontinued—temporarily, according to local accounts—on November 22, 1970. The remote preparation for this service began in the fall of 1968, the proximate preparations in the fall of 1969. The production of the new service was abortive in itself—that is, the service was not sustained. But further experiments occurred after the service itself was discontinued.

The events as they occurred were as follows:

1. The convention demonstrations in August 1968: During the convention, the pastor allowed demonstrators to sleep in the church gymnasium. Shortly after the convention, an associate pastor gave a sermon entitled "The Keystone Cops," which was offensive to some members of the congregation.
2. New personnel were appointed to the Worship and Sacrament Committee in October 1968.
3. The associate pastor with a reputation for being "liberal to radical" left St. Paul for a new position in November 1968.
4. The Worship and Sacrament Committee was reorganized in the fall of 1969, to prepare a "new worship service."
5. The first experimental liturgy was performed on May 3, 1970, with about forty persons in attendance.

6. The last experimental liturgy was performed on November 22, 1970, with five persons in attendance.

7. The Christian Education Committee of St. Paul began using scripture readings as part of its meetings in April 1971.

THE CONVENTION DEMONSTRATIONS

The primary effect of the convention demonstrations on the congregation of St. Paul was to destroy the image of solidarity which up to that time had been held in delicate balance. When the pastor—who was thoroughly respected by the whole congregation—allowed the demonstrators to use the church gym without the prior approval of the Church Council, differences of opinion came to public expression in the congregation. When, furthermore, an associate pastor gave his controversial sermon at the eleven o'clock worship service, the differences of political feeling were even more emphasized.

This fact requires some explanation. The "more liberal" associate pastor had usually preached at the ten o'clock worship service, which was attended by the segment of the congregation which liked his "sermons of involvement." The "more conservative" segment of the congregation attended the eleven o'clock service, partly to avoid the preaching style of the associate pastor. There was also a third service every Sunday, at nine o'clock, which was entirely in German. This *Gottesdienst* was attended by about twenty-five elderly members of the congregation. It continued undisturbed throughout the course of events generated by the convention demonstrations.

The "Keystone Cops" sermon was given at the eleven o'clock worship service, and so the confrontation between different social and political views of members of the congregation was inevitable. This confrontation brought into public focus cleavages of which the congregation was already privately aware and which it had sought to prevent from erupting by constructing separate worship services for members of different opinions.

DEALING WITH DIFFERENCES

The social device selected by the congregation for dealing with the discovery of cleavages in the group was to continue the separation of the congregation into two subcongregations, each with its own worship service. The Worship and Sacrament Committee became the forum of open discussion of the issues central to the cleavages. This committee was formed by the decision of the pastor, who got the approval of the Church Council and asked for volunteers. During the course of the committee's meetings, representatives of the Council and some conservative members of the congregation attended the meetings, but the latter found it difficult to justify and sustain their attendance. One such person stopped attending. He was unable to focus on the precise nature of his discomfort but said, "This group is just not for me. I really don't fit in here."

The Worship and Sacrament Committee devoted its energies to the discussion of changes in the content of the ten o'clock worship service. When the associate pastor resigned his position later in the fall, the group of lay persons who preferred his style of preaching continued their discussions still more privately.

During the year from the fall of 1968 to the fall of 1969, the congregation of St. Paul became organized around the religious styles of four subcongregations. Besides the three already mentioned—the elderly members of the congregation who still preferred to worship in German, the more conservative persons who worshiped in English at eleven o'clock, and the more liberal persons who worshiped at ten o'clock and took part in the Worship and Sacrament Committee—a fourth group developed. This group attended worship service very rarely or not at all and became the nucleus of the Christian Education Committee of St. Paul.

In the fall of 1969 the Worship and Sacrament Committee was reorganized, now with a slightly different mission: to compose a new "experimental" worship service.

DISCUSSING THE NEW RITUAL

The committee met almost every week for seven months. Approximately twenty persons took part in the meetings, the average attendance being ten persons. The coordinator of the Worship and Sacrament Committee was a member of the congregation studying for the ministry at the University of Chicago Divinity School. During the seven months, the members of the committee attended worship services either at ten or eleven o'clock, and at no time during this period did they perform an experimental liturgy. These seven months were therefore a period of "prolonged indecision." Prolonged indecision is a symptom of *conflict,* and apparently the central cause of this indecision was the conflict between self and tradition as the source of sacred ritual.

The conflict in this case was not organizational. The members of the Worship and Sacrament Committee were not so much afraid of offending or not satisfying other members of the congregation of St. Paul as they were unable to avoid offending themselves. The evidence for this is from two sources. One is the organizational procedure by which the committee was set up; the other is the manner in which the members of the committee described, in interviews and in the meetings, their own goals and dissatisfactions.

After he had set up the Worship and Sacrament Committee and found volunteers, the pastor left the committee members to themselves. It was understood that they would develop novelties, but that those novelties would not be imposed on the whole congregation and that the new worship service would not conflict with existing worship services. Thus the committee was structurally free to develop whatever new forms of ritual it thought fit.

But within the committee, its members spent seven months discussing the form the new ritual should take. Just before the experimental worship service was first performed—in May 1970—one of the members commented on how preoccupied with form they had been for the previous six months. The tenor of this comment was supported by other statements. After the new worship service had been performed on several consecutive Sundays, one of the members commented that the group seemed rigidly tied down by the piece of paper on which the order of the ritual was printed. Whenever they stood up to gather around the altar table, they had to have their papers with them, and this seemed to be a great burden. Furthermore, before any order of ritual could actually be performed, the consensus of the whole group was necessary. The group was afraid of "making a mistake": of performing a ritual which was theologically unorthodox. They had to avoid the risk of this kind of error *before* ritual was performed.

The goals of the committee were most frequently stated in negative terms. Its members agreed that they did not like what some of them called the "theatrical" style of preaching of the pastor. They wanted a more conversational style, and group participation in the sermon. They also did not want the presiding clergymen to use vestments: the long robe, clerical collar, and stole whose use is customary in the congregation. On the other hand, they did want a clergyman to perform the initiating role in the communion service (which they used as an integral part of every worship service).

SOME CHARACTERISTICS OF THE
EXPERIMENTAL RITUAL

There was some lack of consistency in the principles of this ritual. On the one hand, the committee did not fully accept the principle that sacred forms are made by authority external to the individual worshiper—that is, "the church," as found in the persons of the clergy who are specially trained and symbolically "set aside" from lay persons. On the other hand, they did not accept that the individual lay person should have immediate contact with the sacred, and that the ritual should be composed out of the spontaneous expressive forms arising from individual members of the Worship and Sacrament Committee, these contributions being valid enough to be tested by the group through ritual *performance*. That is, they did not accept either of these principles *operationally*. Although the stated ideology of the group tended to affirm the priesthood of all believers, the practice of the group did not express this principle.

Thus the group lost the solemnity, security, and consistency which come from accepting external authority's authenticity in defining the sacred cosmos. It also lost the experience of discovering the sacred in the authenticity of another person's spontaneous contributions—which appears to be the central meaning of interaction ritual—because the members of the committee were not able to take themselves or the other members seriously as sources of expressive forms of the sacred.

Therefore, from the beginning of May through the summer of 1970 and on into the fall, the group performed rituals in various places (a classroom, the church chapel, the church lawn) and at various times (Sunday morning, Sunday evening, weekday evenings), with steadily decreasing attendance, from approximately forty persons in May to only five in November. One member of the committee who attended the services on and off for about three months could not pinpoint the difficulty but summarized her disappointment by saying, "It lacks authenticity."

ANOTHER EXPERIMENT

During the fall of 1970, just as the experimental ritual of the Worship and Sacrament Committee was being terminated, the meetings of the Christian Education Committee were giving rise to an increasingly coherent criticism of the religious style of the congregation of St. Paul. After the experimental worship service was discontinued, some persons who had formed the nucleus of the Worship and Sacrament Committee began attending meetings of the Christian Education Committee.

The formal purpose of this committee was to plan the curriculum and teaching schedules of the church school, which met on Sunday mornings.[13] The committee's commitment to Christian education quickly gave rise to discussion of the religious styles of adults. Sometime in the winter of 1970–71, the members of the Christian Education Committee discovered that although all of them were serious about religion, almost none ever attended worship service. During this time, too, a proposal was made that the committee include a reading from the Bible and some discussion of that reading as an integral part of their meetings. It was pointed out that such a practice would be "ersatz ritual" and make them an "ersatz church." The committee instituted the practice nonetheless.

The members of the Christian Education Committee became increasingly aware of differences between their own religious styles and what they perceived to be the style of the majority or the "center" of the congregation. In the spring of 1971 they began to consider ways of introducing issues which they felt were healthily controversial into the public life of the whole congregation. Therefore they began planning to make proposals at the spring meeting of St. Paul's Session, the principal legislative body of the congregation, composed of approximately 200 persons. At the time of writing they had decided to make only one proposal at the meeting, and that would be a formal proposal, to be debated and voted upon, that the Session be abolished.

The members of the Christian Education Committee were more interested in the debate than they were in the vote. They did not expect to win if their resolution came to a vote. They were, rather, looking for a device to raise to public consideration the authentic

---

[13] I participated in teaching the junior high section of the magnet church school during the 1969–1970 school year. This school drew children from five local congregations—including St. Paul—and met on Thursday afternoons.

differences in religious style in the congregation. In the previous two years these differences had been inchoately raised several times but had never been brought to public resolution.[14]

Here again it seems correct to say that the process of making differences public for the collectivity means making them conscious for the individual members. The majority of the congregation apparently still resisted this event.

This resistance to theological differences seems to be characteristic of congregations which prefer worshiping in mass ritual. Interaction ritual handles such differences differently. Its function is to stimulate and try to resolve them, not by means of common formulas but by emphasizing the process of finding formulas as central to religious commitment. This kind of ritual expresses not a set of meanings that are common and fixed but a process of continually revising meanings by interaction.

SUMMARY AND CONCLUSIONS

The transition from mass ritual to interaction ritual is a process of transferring responsibility for creating global meaning from the authority of traditional and official institutions to the authority of individual persons gathered in an interacting group. At many points in the multisided conversation of interaction ritual, the agreements and disagreements of members of the group are dramatized and celebrated. These are the moments when interaction ritual looks most like mass ritual: a song is sung, a sermon listened to, a prayer recited. But these common group activities are but points in a more funda-

[14] Without making a claim for universality, it is still encouraging to find corroborating testimony from unexpected sources. A minister writes: "For seven years, no matter how we attempted to involve the congregation, the physical arrangement still prevailed, and the people remained an audience rather than a worshiping community acting out a drama." After seven years of failure—and I would be glad to know the method and quality of the exegetical input—they tried a "restaging." The minister comments: "The experiment was not without some trepidation and some controversy, for the spectator disposition was stronger than we thought." (William Holmes, *Tomorrow's Church: A Cosmopolitan Community* [New York: Abingdon Press, 1968], p. 78.)

I would comment: (1) there would have been no trepidation if latent meanings had been changed; (2) the delayed awareness—seven years—is to be expected; (3) as long as the initiative for change remains with the clergy—as it did in this case—the order of changes in exegetical, latent, and hidden meanings can be disrupted in many ways. Only when the initiative resides in the community does the "natural" progression from conscious to unconscious systems remain intact.

mental process, the process of discovering agreements and disagreements. Persons who are moved by interaction ritual are moved by the process of creating meaning with others and not simply by the dramatizations of momentary unanimity. They relish the sharing of charisma.

From the two instances we have just described, the transition from mass ritual to interaction ritual appears to have five empirical characteristics. The first three of these confirm and explicate its nature as a shift in the social location of authority for creating global meaning. These three are (1) the occurrence of resistance and anxiety in the initial stage of the transition, (2) the changing basis of affiliation and solidarity in the group undergoing the transition, and (3) the place of controversy in the process. A fourth characteristic—the limits of community experienced in the complete transition in the Church of the Three Crosses—indicates that the range of meanings criticized by interaction ritual is limited by social, historical, and cultural circumstances. A fifth characteristic—the piecemeal nature of the transition—seems to be a manifestation of the social-psychological structure of symbol systems in general. They are organic and gestaltic wholes, yet are composed of discrete parts and multilayered in their levels of meaning.

Resistance and Anxiety

Resistance to change and anxiety in the process of transition occurred in both of the instances I have described. In the Church of the Three Crosses, the suggestion of change produced meetings "with a lot of yelling," followed by a euphoric resolution of the tension in a renewed sense of community. The converging testimony of events says that the source of anxiety is over the transfer of authority from tradition to self. This is most clear in the controversy about changing the hour of worship, but it is also shown in persons' feelings about many issues of "form," such as formal prayers. This is the issue of *traditional* form. Once religious believers decide that they do indeed have the authority to create a symbol system, "form" becomes a secondary issue; the form of the ritual undergoes rapid and seemingly disordered changes, and participants are content with such disorder as long as there is "authenticity." "Form" in this context designates a system of *fixed relationships* among symbols. The "form" of a formal prayer is such because it is unchanging.

In the experimental ritual of St. Paul, this preoccupation with form was a symptom of the fundamental ambivalence and indecision of the participants as regards two conflicting sources of authority: the institution of the church, with its traditions and its hierarchy, on the one hand, and the charismatic self of religious believers, on the other. It would seem in this context that one cannot serve two masters. In creating a public ritual, participants must choose one or the other source of authority. The year-long discussion of form in the committee of St. Paul Church symptomizes the indecision arising from the anxiety caused by the difficulty of this choice. Only in the "ersatz ritual" of the Christian Education Committee was the choice apparently made, but the making of that choice put the members of that committee in such opposition to the majority of the congregation that it had not been resolved at the time of this writing.

The Changing Basis of Affiliation

The process of transition from mass ritual to interaction ritual requires a degree of personal intimacy not required in hierarchically structured congregations. The initial call for a twofold "involvement" in the Church of the Three Crosses (involvement of the congregation in the community outside its own traditional and "natural" boundaries, and of the lay members of the congregation in the sacred tasks of the clergy) is a call for interpersonal community. It means the dissolution of mere role-specific relationships in favor of "diffuse" relationships. Both "ascriptive" and "achievement-based" classifications of persons are challenged in this call, in favor of purely personal judgments. The chief basis of community is no longer commitment to the same objective symbol system but a sharing of a common psychic ("spiritual") labor, that of constructing meaningful relationships between individuals and various elements of their environment. Such bases of community as socioeconomic status, ethnicity, traditional religious affiliation, race, and even language are declared to be progressively less relevant to the common bonds which hold the community together. Ascriptive and achievement-based judgments of persons assign status to individuals on the basis of nonpersonal attributes. Ascription looks to a person's birth, and achievement looks to a person's performance in the material productive system. They are not intrinsically moral or personal. These "secondary" bases of social affiliation are of course very important for the original association of the persons in the group that performs interaction ritual. But in the process of creating that ritual, the biographies of the participants are so fully publicized that each becomes classified and judged on such qualities as openness, honesty, willingness to listen, and the disposition to change one's mind.

The Place of Controversy

In the process of transition from mass ritual to interaction ritual, the group tends to cultivate controversy. This is because the community of interaction ritual is not based on any assumed "likeness of kind," as expressed, for instance, in the statement "We are all Lutherans, aren't we?" In fact, it assumes just the opposite: that each participant is unique and therefore different from everyone else. (We all recognize each other's charisma, don't we?) Individuals are encouraged to say what they "really" think, whether or not their opinions promise to be in conformity with others'. Disagreements are aired both about religious topics—such as the suitability of prayers or hymns—and about secular topics—such as the activities of the Black Panthers, the actions of demonstrators, the position on urban renewal taken by community organizations. This encouragement of self-expression also implies encouragement of self-examination and self-criticism, because where the uniqueness of individuals is emphasized, differences are bound to occur. The cultivation of controversy leads to a continuous tendency for persons to criticize the taken-for-granted bases of personal choices in many spheres of social life. This process requires expenditures of energy not typically required of members of a stable social and cultural system.

Controversy in this context is a process of applying common principles to different concrete contexts of behavior and action. This process of discovering meaning is so important in the transition from mass ritual to interaction ritual and in interaction ritual itself that it becomes central to the religion. The discussions and arguments in the meetings of the worship task force are "where worship happens" for members of the Church of the Three Crosses. *Working out* meanings is the essential task of religion in this view.

The Limits of Community

In the transition occurring in the Church of the Three Crosses, the congregation on two occasions (in 1965 and in 1970) discussed the form of "commitment" expressed in the sharing of incomes and living in the same household. On both occasions the group decided that economic sharing and communal living were not forms of community they could undertake.

The process of transition from mass ritual to interaction ritual increases the participants' awareness of one another as distinct persons. It seems clear that persons participating in mass ritual together can still perceive one another as total strangers. In agreeing to share the process of constructing ritual, believers agree to tell one another things about themselves that are relevant to that process, such as the elements of their personal biographies which influence their personal interpretations of religious symbols. Thus persons who set about constructing ritual together get to know one another personally in a way which is not necessary for participation in mass ritual. This increase in mutual personal knowledge leads to feelings of increased intimacy, which is part of a process characterized by social inertia: it tends to remain in motion until stopped by an opposing force. It was therefore logical for the members of the Church of the Three Crosses—having become intimates where once they were strangers—to discuss openly how far they wanted the process to go. The fact that they decided to stop at the kind of commitment expressed in worship task force meetings, in sharing in congregational committees, in occasional parties, and on Sunday mornings, indicates that they wanted a mutual dependence beyond that required by mass ritual but less than that expressed in other forms of community, such as the sharing of incomes and living in the same household.

Thus it is clear that the transition from mass ritual to interaction ritual changes the basis of social relationships for its participants, but in a specific and limited way. They move from being strangers to being intimates, but maintain certain spheres of independence and privacy.

The Piecemeal Nature of the Process

Mass ritual, as noted, does not change to interaction ritual all at once but gradually, by means of a series of decisions. In the transitions discussed, the change of the hour of worship, introduction of a secular reading, use of the guitar, dropping of certain prayers, putting up of new decorations, and rearrangement of furniture were all particular decisions which were made because they seemed appropriate at the time. Moreover, the members of the Church of the Three Crosses did not have the end of the process clearly in view when they began to change their "understanding" of ritual in 1964. In this sense, the transition from mass ritual to interaction ritual is a "natural process." Even if it is not planned, it has a natural starting point, a natural terminus, and natural phases between start and finish. In retrospect, the particular decisions made at particular times because they seemed appropriate show a pattern.

First, the organic whole of the new form of ritual begins as inarticulate dissatisfaction with the current form of ritual: "There was gonna have to be some redirection in this congregation." The original call for change in the Church of the Three Crosses was for more "involvement" of the congregation in the ritual and of the congregation in the life of the neighborhood.

Second, the process of change proceeds by focusing on discrete elements of the ritual. An organically new form of ritual is arrived at by a series of particular changes, such as changing the time for worship, introducing a new operation such as the secular reading, introducing the guitar, dropping a certain series of prayers, and so forth.

Third, the series of changes leading to a new form proceeds from the most conscious level of meaning of ritual to the most unconscious level. That is, interpretations change first, then motor activity, then spatial arrangements. There is overlap among these three levels in that, after new interpretations of ritual have been expressed, they are expanded and revised along with changes in the operational meanings of ritual. During this middle phase of change, all three levels of meaning may be experimented with. But the expressions of the hidden meanings of ritual in spatial arrangements will always lag behind. The final phase of change brings the spatial arrangements of ritual into harmony with the completed changes in interpretation and patterns of motor activity.

Fourth, the process of change is initiated and sustained by charismatic input. This is charisma in the strict sociological sense of the opposition of personal authority to institutional authority: "It is written, but I say. . . ." It may indeed happen that the charismatic aspect of the change will eventually be routinized, but in order for the organic unity of a current institutional pattern to be dissolved in favor of a new pattern, the intervention of charismatic authority is required. In the changes we have discussed, the principal difference between the Church of the Three Crosses and St. Paul Church was in respect to the occurrence of charisma. In the Church of the Three Crosses, charisma was provided by the co-ministers. They went ahead on their own authority. Granted that they retained the approval of a liberal denominational hierarchy, they still persuaded the institutional church to make innovations whose value they alone saw. This is the meaning of the seemingly simple innovation of the co-pastorate. They persuaded the church to approve it, and they persuaded the congregation to accept it. In the changes which occurred in St. Paul, on the other hand, no single member of the group suggested that the authority of the church be set aside, even "for the moment" or "just to see what will happen." Rather, the potentially personal and charismatic authority of their suggestions for changes was inhibited by their identification with institutional authority. Their concern for "form" is the principal evidence of this.

If we accept religious ritual as a specimen of culture—that is, of a symbol system embedded in social reality, giving meaning to that reality—then we may see in the patterns of the change of a religious ritual a possible paradigm for other forms of cultural change. In particular, charismatic authority may be seen as the mediating authority between institutionally legitimized cultural syntheses. Also, if cultures always tend to be organically unified and complete, experimentalism and syncretism in cultural and social behavior may be signs not only of movement away from prior culture but of movement toward new syntheses.

CHAPTER 10

Ritual and Change

In the preceding chapters we have developed the argument that in the middle-class congregations studied it is very important to make the distinction between mass ritual and interaction ritual, based on a structural analysis of Sunday morning worship services. The central sociological significance of this distinction is that it points to a shift in the social location of meaning-giving and moral authority for worshipers in a mainline denomination and therefore to an underlying and fundamental aspect of religious change in contemporary society.

In the present chapter we shall review the argument in a condensed and summary fashion and consider some of its implications.

MASS RITUAL AS USUAL

Mass ritual is the usual form of religious ritual in organized religions. In three of the four churches we examined, mass ritual was the dominant accepted form of worship service.

The reasons for the continued predominance of mass ritual surely have something to do with the fact that it emphasizes the stability of social hierarchy and continuity with the past and so resists the definition of a situation as anomic. The separation of the sacred cosmos from the profane world gives the sacred an enduring and stable quality above the fluctuations and relative chaos of the meanings of everyday life. By centralizing the production of religious meanings, mass ritual fits well into the fabric of a society in which institutions are stable and the meaning of everyday life is adequately defined by traditional and official symbol systems.

Interaction ritual, on the other hand, is a ritual of fluid boundaries between the sacred and the profane and so emphasizes the process of continually constructing the relationship between them. It accepts the problematic issues and events which create a situation of anomie and becomes an intuitive and charismatic process to integrate such a situation into a new meaningful synthesis.

LINCOLN PARK AS ANOMIC SITUATION

The situation in Lincoln Park in the late 1960s was potentially anomic. In considering this point, we should recall that anomie is a collective representation, not an objective property of historical events. Therefore, it is the result of an interpretation of events. Clearly, some residents of Lincoln Park interpreted the events of the sixties as comprising an anomic situation and others did not.

One source of anomie was the civil rights movement. The militant demonstrations of the mid-sixties challenged the legitimacy of customary American ways of organizing relationships between blacks and whites. As laws began to change and behavior proved to be more difficult to change, the location of the problem in the cultural phenomenon of *custom* became clearer to some religious believers. For those who doubted the justice of such customs, a source of meaning was called into question.

The civil rights movement touched Chicago closely in the mid-sixties through the open-housing marches led by Martin Luther King. It touched Lincoln Park indirectly but profoundly through the presence of a huge public-housing project on its southern boundary, which sent large numbers of black students to the main public high school of Lincoln Park and provided a population base for strong migratory pressure northward.

For many in the area, this situation was not anomic; it was just dangerous. The principle of conduct was clear: keep them out. The problem was merely technical: how to keep them out. For the few persons labeled radicals, the situation was also not anomic. For them, too, the principle was clear: let them in. For them, too, the problem of civil rights was a technical one: how to keep the poor and minority ethnic groups in the area.

For still another group of persons, the situation was indeed anomic. On the one hand, they could not appeal to tradition and custom, because to them the morality of these institutions was clearly wrong. Nor could they look to Marxist ideology, because they had never been convincingly exposed to it, and they also thought that Christianity was sufficient. As urban renewal got under way, the anomie deepened, because it also became clear that they could not use lobbying and personal influence to change the policies of legitimate authorities, for those techniques were controlled by a coalition of interests whose goals were seen as purely pragmatic and selfish.

Thus government and the powerful institutions of the community did not provide any moral authority to help resolve the demands of substantive justice. This in turn meant that the policies and pronouncements of government could not be seen as a source of valid meaning of the events in the community.

In the midst of urban renewal there were strident and conflicting claims by parties who said that justice and "the people" were on their side. The Young Lords Organization and the Concerned Citizens Survival Front put the issues in Marxist rhetoric. The Lincoln Park Conservation Association castigated its opponents as radicals and troublemakers. There was a group in the middle which could not accept either of these positions. For this group these strident voices were also devoid of meaning-giving authority. Thus a certain group of religious believers were left with an anomic situation in which they themselves were the only possible source of meaning.

At the same time that these secular events were taking place, some believers were already experimenting with a new ritual, designed to get them more involved in the community around them and to get lay people more involved in worship. This interaction ritual crystallized into a stable form of religious worship, becoming a cultural blueprint: a model of the world, and a model for social action.

Many other Christians in the community were worshiping in mass ritual. This form of ritual, too, served as a cultural blueprint. As religious believers responded to the events of the late sixties, many of them had these cultural blueprints with them in the form of the worship services they attended regularly on Sunday mornings.

THE INTACT MORAL ORDER

The participants in mass ritual tended to see the moral order in Lincoln Park as fundamentally intact. These religious believers did not see social problems as religious ones. Their position regarding such issues as the morality of the activities of the Black Panther party, for example, was that they did not know, they could not say, they would have to wait for the analysis of experts. The church could not advise the faithful on how to act in regard to these difficult problems. Even discussion of them would be fruitless, for no one would have enough information to provide a definitive solution.

In the demonstrations of 1968, our four churches behaved very differently. The Church of the Three Crosses became deeply involved: by housing demonstrators, housing the Medical Commission for Human Rights, actually going to the park to try to mediate. The liberal minister of St. Paul housed demonstrators in the church gym and received the criticism of the Church Council for doing so. St. James and St. Clement refused requests to house demonstrators. Their pastors said that the events were really not their business; individual believers could make their own moral judgments, but the morality of the situation was not of concern to the church. The moral order upheld by the religion of these churches was not affected by these social upheavals. Such troublesome events remained outside the pale of the intact moral order portrayed in mass ritual.

TRADITION, OFFICE, AND CHARISMA

The transition from mass ritual to interaction ritual expresses a shift from tradition and office to charisma—that is, the personal power (and responsibility) of each participant in the worship—as the source of moral authority. Interaction ritual is an attempt to institutionalize the dispersal, or sharing, of charisma. It assumes that all participants have equal access to the sacred—which is the source of ultimate meanings—and therefore that all have equal authority to contribute to the meaning-giving activity which is the purpose of the group's ritual.

The interaction ritual we observed in the Church of the Three Crosses does not totally eliminate tradition or office as the source of authority, but it sharply reduces their power in the process of finding meanings. Tradition remains in the readings from the Bible and the indebtedness to a denominational past of members of the congregation. Each person in the ritual comes from some "tradition." Office remains in that there are clergy in the congregation. But their principal responsibility becomes not teaching, but bureaucratic logistics. They keep things organized and do the many administrative tasks necessary to keep the building open, books balanced, schedules printed, and so forth.

Mass ritual, on the other hand, produces meanings on the basis of tradition and office. The authority to make meaning is invested principally in tradition and the clergy. Thus mass ritual is the ritual of hierarchy and centralization. The mass rituals we observed dealt with charisma in various ways. That is, they had different levels of tolerance. But even those most open to charisma still think it exceptional and center their meaning-giving activity on the authority of tradition and office. In mass ritual the sacred is enclosed in such a way that there is limited access to it. Meaning is produced in an orderly way.

Religious believers attend both kinds of ritual. For each set of believers, the worship service is a celebration. But each form of ritual celebrates different things. Interaction ritual celebrates a community of equals and says in effect that in the last analysis you are dependent on yourself. Mass ritual celebrates tradition and office. It celebrates each participant's connection with the center. There is joy in the order of things. In the last analysis, it says, you are dependent on the Lord, his Book, and his church.

STRUCTURES, EXPERIENCE, HISTORY

Those who took part in interaction ritual did so partly because they were not connected with structural vehicles of tradition: ethnicity, strong criteria of orthodoxy, centralized organization, and economic security. In addition, they had personal or vicarious experiences with the emptiness of office and tradition. It seems that these phenomena support one another: marginality with respect to the structural vehicles of tradition supports disaffection from the authority of tradition and office, and disaffection supports a disavowal of one's affiliation with the structural vehicles of tradition. Finally, the Church of the Three Crosses was heir to a tradition of populism, dormant until this reawakening.

In 1964 the congregation of the Church of the Three Crosses had a weak allegiance to tradition, the product of a complex mixture of factors. In the late 1960s this congregation had no well-knit ethnic tradition, such as that of the Missouri Synod of the Lutheran Church. The members of the church came from many different ethnic backgrounds. The congregation belonged to an old denomination—the Evangelical United Brethren—whose traditions were vaguely populist and nonhierarchical. The EUB had been the church of rural and small-town believers who valued inspirational preaching more than learning and doctrinal authority. In this respect they differed sharply from their sister church in the United Church of Christ, St. Paul, whose antecedents lay in urban, affluent, and educated German Lutheranism. Organizationally, the Church of the Three Crosses shared with other Protestant congregations a tradition of local autonomy, and in this respect it differed from the Roman Catholic church in our study. Furthermore, the Church of the Three Crosses saw itself as a "dying church," which meant that its members admitted the possibility of the extinction of the church through loss of members or income. In all the other churches in our study, the validity of tradition and of office was supported by one or more of these structural vehicles.

The transition from mass ritual to interaction ritual was initiated by two ministers who were co-pastors of the Church of the Three Crosses from 1964 to 1970. They drew members of the congregation into a process whose end they did not clearly see. They only saw the need for a twofold "involvement": of the congregation in the liturgy and of the church in the community. Yet the process was indeed the cultivation and dispersal of charisma, and it did in fact end in interaction ritual. It was a process of several years of face-to-face conversation between the co-pastors and others in the church. Therefore, the co-pastors' experiences with the emptiness of office and tradition contributed heavily to the emergence of interaction ritual here. Their being uprooted from commitment to office and tradition infiltrated the whole congregation.

When the co-pastors were asked how they came to view a new kind of ritual as necessary, they cited elements of their biographies. Each had had certain experiences in childhood and adolescence, in the seminary, and in Lincoln Park which made "involvement" a very important concept for him. The experiences they mentioned can be summarized under four headings: (1) commitment to Christianity as a valid religious symbol system, (2) personal experience with and rejection of institutionalized racism as an American custom, (3) assessment of the social life of traditionalist religious congregations as trivial and superficial, and (4) personal experience with the powerlessness of the poor in the face of official governmental policies.

The co-pastors and some other members of the Church of the Three Crosses spoke of childhood experiences in which they perceived their parents to be committed Christians and otherwise reasonable, loving, humane persons. A warm family background is not common to all members of the congregation, but it was mentioned by some as a source of their enduring commitment to Christianity as a flexible and meaningful symbol system. What *is* common to all the members of the congregation is that, for whatever reasons, they shared the conviction that the teachings of Christ and of the Bible have an enduring and profound significance with regard to the moral interpretation of events of everyday life.

Awareness of racism also figures in the formation of interaction ritual. One of the ministers in question spoke of his early discovery of the racial boundaries in his hometown as a significant formative experience. My inference from his and other members' descriptions of their lives is that there is a specific logic to the connection between experience with racism and commitment to interaction ritual. Institutionalized racism—as expressed, for example, in the custom which forbids blacks to be in a certain section of a small town after dark—is rooted in custom. If racism is perceived as unjust, then the injustice can be attributed to no particular person or agency. To the question why it occurs, the usual and most accurate answer is simply "That's the way things are done around here." Institutionalized racism draws its power precisely from being *customary*. However, customs are cultural phenomena, made not by one person or group who can be blamed for the bad ones but by a complex process of formation of and acquiescence to tradition. If customs are bad and are made by "society," then society itself is to blame. Therefore, in the process of declaring customs evil, traditions and the wisdom of our forefathers are called into question. Against the authority of tradition there are only two possible appeals. One is to the authority of office, and the other is to the authority of charisma. Where the holders of office vacillate or uphold the authority of tradition, the only appeal is to charisma. This authority of charisma is the personal authority of one who finds custom wrong and/or meaningless.

Thus the cultural logic of antiracism moves immediately into a challenge of the authority of tradition and office. This challenge can include ecclesiastical and religious as well as social and secular tradition, if the churches side with custom. The challenge inevitably tends to the cultivation of purely personal ways of finding meaning:

meditation and introspection, self-criticism, and open argumentation with persons willing to argue and to change. Such activities constitute interaction ritual.

Personal experience with racism in the Church of the Three Crosses was combined with vicarious experience obtained through the experiences of friends and media reports. The changes in ritual in this church began in 1964, before the civil rights movement reached its peak of notoriety. The congregation sent two of its members to the civil rights march in Selma, Alabama, in the summer of 1965. They represented the congregation and reported back to it. The members were very attentive to reports of incidents and demonstrations and frequently brought these reports into the ritual itself by reading articles from newspapers immediately before or after readings from the Bible.

My conversations with the participants in interaction ritual also touched on the quality of social life in churches they had known in the past. On this topic many of them became eloquent. Their experience centered on two phenomena: (1) churchgoers never argued with one another in public, and (2) the conversation at church meetings and informal gatherings was exclusively concerned with social trivia, never with important issues. These phenomena merge to form the perception that the social life of churchgoers with one another is hardly ever serious. If there are disagreements, they cannot be raised in a church meeting but must be pushed into private discussions or gripe sessions in "rump groups." The result is that church gatherings are serene and empty.

On the basis of this negative experience, the participants in interaction ritual in the Church of the Three Crosses sought to cultivate controversy and to regard anger as a symptom of authentic religious concern. Their intuition that controversy and anger are essential to authentic religious process could only be based on the assumption that religious interpretation of everyday life is difficult and so requires the serious personal involvement which anger expresses. The legitimation of controversy in group discourse is essentially antihierarchical, for it suspends judgment on the question of who might be right in a disagreement over the interpretation of religious symbols.

The final aspect of the social sources of interaction ritual is the powerlessness of the poor. For the members of the Church of the Three Crosses, urban renewal was the principal expression of this powerlessness. They interpreted urban renewal as "urban removal": keeping or pushing out blacks, Puerto Ricans, and poor whites from the Lincoln Park area. Urban renewal was for them a coalition of powerful political and economic vested interests whose concerns were selfish and not humane. As they took part in the struggle over the percentage of low-income housing to be included in the plan for the area, they became more and more disaffected from the principles that seemed to undergird the political and economic system of government. The meaning of urban renewal for them was different from its meaning for the powerful. There was therefore a selective affinity between their style of religious ritual and their opposition to official programs for urban renewal. In ritual they depended on themselves to discover religious meanings, not on the authority of religious hierarchs.[1] In social policy, too, they insisted on the rightness and authenticity of their own interpretations and did not accept the programs of the powerful and the experts. In both ritual and social policy, they opposed the authenticity of self (and we-group) to the authority of tradition and bureaucratic office.

Granted that the occurrence of interaction ritual is a shift in the social location of meaning-giving authority for its participants, we may still ask what significance this shift has in reference to other social processes. How important is the change from mass ritual to interaction ritual in this one small church in Lincoln Park?

LINCOLN PARK AS MICROCOSM

The situation in Lincoln Park in the late 1960s in a sense mirrored the potential anomie of the United States as a whole beginning with the national agony over the Vietnam war. The interactive and symbolic strategies devised by residents of Lincoln Park in response to their community crisis are models of such strategies for all members of the industralized West.

It is not that the phenomenon of interaction ritual is new. I have mentioned its previous appearance in the form of the Quaker meeting, for example. The interaction ritual which occurred in Lincoln Park in the late 1960's is only one form of the current of mysticism and charisma which always flows along with tradition and official authority in the organization of societies.

---

[1] The congregation also took part in the Renewal Caucus of the United Methodist Church. This caucus acted as a popular lobby, often disagreeing with denominational executives and the majority of the denomination council. They acted on the center from the periphery.

When great cultural syntheses break up, they do so gradually
and with the accompaniment of many fractionated outbursts of
the mystical inclination of the human spirit. The mystical poten-
tiality is the avenue by which humankind reaches back into the
unconscious for new grounds of moral order when traditional bases
for such order lose their credibility and legitimacy. One response
to the situation in which traditional and conventional definitions of
morality no longer satisfy is a combination of fear and anger at the
overthrow of what was once so good and valuable.

> . . . it is no paradox that a society which has, helter skelter, been abandon-
> ing its traditional Judaeo-Christian heritage is now producing demons.
> And to say that it has found no way of controlling them is to ignore
> the reasons our "free and liberal society" is continuing to produce them
> in ever-greater numbers. . . . The parents, teachers and professors of
> today's Youth Rebels were in their cradles when the intellectuals pro-
> claimed "the death of God," the "Old Man" of the entire Judaeo-Chris-
> tian tribe, and began to scrap the moral standards by which Western
> society had judged right and wrong, good and bad, desirable and un-
> desirable conduct for centuries.[2]

This kind of defense of the past often looks for villains and
scapegoats in the movement of cultural change. The sense of opposition that develops between protagonists of tradition and protagonists
of new moral systems is potentially volatile. One reason is that the
defense of tradition is often a defense of traditional privilege. But
there is also a deep-seated psychic conflict between the comforts
of legitimate moral hierarchy and the uncertainties of self-direction.
Our data on church rituals in Lincoln Park show how some of the
conflicts over the obsolescence of tradition can be resolved in an
orderly and humane manner.

But interaction ritual is only one of many options in a time
of cultural reconstruction. To understand where it fits in the larger
picture, we should backtrack a little and look at its relationship
to the most recent major upheaval in Western religion: the Protestant Reformation.

THE ECLIPSE OF PROTESTANTISM

Robert Bellah says that specialist and hierarchical religious roles
emerged in the "archaic" stage of religious evolution, continued
in the stage of "historic" religion, and began to break down in the

[2] Clare Booth Luce, "The Significance of Squeaky Fromme," *Wall Street
Journal*, September 24, 1975, p. 2.

"early modern" religion of the Protestant Reformation.[3] But my data show that the operational meaning of Protestant ritual is contrary to Luther's theological pronouncement of the priesthood of all believers. What Bellah calls the "usual reservations and mortgages to the past" of the Protestant breakthrough are so powerful that in most cases of Protestant religious practice the breakthrough has long since been canceled out.

The original protest of Protestantism was against the authority of the pope and the hierarchy implicit in allegiance to the papacy. Mass ritual re-creates the substance of that moral hierarchy with the inclusion of different personnel in the authoritative roles. Thus Bellah's assertion that Protestantism has "successfully institutionalized the system of immediate salvation" is just not true. The fiscal and organizational autonomy of congregations notwithstanding, there is today the same kind of meaning-giving authority in Protestantism as there is in Roman Catholicism. And this has probably been the case ever since Luther's retrenchment on his preaching of nonhierarchical religious authority at the time of the Peasants' Revolt.

The Protestant Reformation, from this perspective, emerges as an extremely important reorganization of religious polity in the West; but it was not, finally, a populist or popular resistance to centralized, hierarchical moral authority. In the early stages of the formation of many Protestant groups, the paradigm of shifting the social location of moral authority from established hierarchs to local we-groups was certainly followed. But in the face of growing nationalism and growing bureaucratization, this paradigm succumbed to the overwhelming force of secular developments. The spark was ignited, but the institutional climate was not ready for it to flame. As some of the data from this study eloquently show, for most individual believers, Protestantism has meant exchanging the pope in Rome for a pope at home.

It would seem that the common authority structure of Protestantism and Roman Catholicism is the source of the common difficulties both forms of religion are experiencing at the present time.

INTERACTION RITUAL AS A SOCIAL MOVEMENT

Narrowly viewed, interaction ritual is a form of institutionalized religious ritual, occurring in the context of church membership.

[3] Robert N. Bellah, "Religious Evolution," *American Sociological Review* 29 (June 1964): 358–74.

Broadly viewed, it is a social strategy of we-groups for institution-alizing the authority of shared charisma. To judge whether inter-action ritual is a social movement we must look at it both ways.

The only way to answer this question definitively is to do em-pirical research on the matter. But on the basis of the present work, I have a two-part hypothesis as to what empirical studies will find. I think they will find that interaction ritual in the narrow sense is not a social movement. They will find that it occurs temporarily and sporadically, in concrete forms which try to mix hierarchical and shared charismatic authority, but not consistently and cumula-tively within the boundaries of established religious organizations. I also think empirical studies will find that interaction ritual in the broad sense is, albeit weak, a nascent social movement.

Mass ritual is the usual form of worship in organized religions. Even in the relatively troubled Lincoln Park of the late 1960s, only three of the forty-four churches moved very far in the direction of interaction ritual. When I revisited the Church of the Three Crosses in 1973, I found that a new pastor had restored elements of mass ritual to the worship service. All utterance and movement were initiated by the pastor and his wife, and a reading stand had been placed in the center of the ritual place, which turned out to be the official position of the minister during the service.

Organized religion is deeply imbued with the belief in sacred hierarchy. When we consider one of the forms the women's move-ment has taken within churches, we can understand this well. The demand by women to be ordained to the priesthood should be welcomed by those churches that wish to preserve the substance of the traditional theology which gives them a reason for existence; for this demand is founded on a belief in sacred hierarchy, the only theoretical foundation for churches as they are known in the West. The logic of feminism could just as well deny the need for priests of either sex.

Church organizations have as much flexibility as any large corpora-tion for liberalizing relations of authority within them while still preserving their essential function. But there is a logic to the transi-tion from mass ritual to interaction ritual which suggests that dis-covering interaction ritual will more likely lead people to leave organized religion than provoke changes in church organization. For the individual believer, the psychic experience associated with a change in the social location of meaning-giving and moral au-thority from external sources to self must strongly tend to raise the question of why *any* affiliation with a church is necessary or desirable. Persons who find interaction ritual to be an authentic expression of their religious beliefs cannot continue to believe in sacred hierarchy. Thus their commitment to a religious organization must move to other grounds, of which there are many.

Churches have considerable economic resources. They are sources of employment. They are usually the basis for webs of friendship and kin ties which function as community for church members. Thus there are many social, as distinct from religious, factors which can make for church affiliation and church attendance. But if the specifically religious basis of affiliation and attendance is consciously disavowed, then a central aspect of the individual's tie to the organization is also weakened.

If the interaction ritual I observed in Lincoln Park is indeed a manifestation of a broader cultural trend, then the future of established church organizations will take shape around their critically important decisions on how to structure sacred authority. It is theoretically possible for a religious organization to abandon sacred hierarchy. But this appears to be extraordinarily difficult and would radically alter the official structure of churches as we know them in the West today. Moreover, the Protestantism which began with the concept of the priesthood of all believers has generally gone in quite the other direction since 1517.

If the probability seems low for a growth in interaction ritual within the churches, its development outside the churches may be more likely, for the meaning-giving process which is the essence of interaction ritual has rather widespread support in the industrial West. There may indeed be a serious contradiction in this culture between its commitment to open-ended meaning systems and its commitment to intractable hierarchies. The contradiction is not resolved but seems in fact to be in the process of ripening.

SURVIVING A CRISIS OF CULTURE

It would be very difficult to devise an adequate definition of a crisis of culture. For the purpose of the present discussion, we need only accept the fact that what is going on these days is not a case of one defective institution, such as government or the family or the educational system or the churches. The authority of *all* institutions is in a state of weakness. The implication of this observation is that there is something behind, or above, all of them which is in a state of perilous decline. This "something" is what I'd like to call—for the sake of opening up a question—culture. It is what Clare Booth Luce called the "traditional Judaeo-Christian heritage."

As has been shown, in making the transition from mass ritual to interaction ritual, a person shifts the social location of meaning-giving and moral authority away from the institutionalized representatives of tradition and official hierarchy to a self acting within a we-group. But the two movements—*away from* and *to*—are distinct and separable. One can move *away from* tradition and official hierarchy *to* other social locations of meaning-giving and moral authority than the charismatic selves of interaction ritual. One can move, for example, to a guru, to the form of consciousness stimulated by hallucinogenic drugs, to a spiritual movement with a single charismatic leader and numerous devoted followers, to a declaration of the irrelevance of issues of morality, to disaffiliation from all religious groups in favor of personal meditation and moral solitude, to enthusiastic support of a demagogue, or to some other form of traditional religion than the present dissatisfying one. Arrival at any of these destinations except the last requires the same exodus: away from the social location of moral authority in tradition and official hierarchies. Once you leave, you're on your own. This is the dangerous situation which is open to creative and destructive possibilities.

No one except a prophet volunteers to oppose a received cultural consensus. All of the prophets of Israel died violent deaths. That's how hard it is. But today we do not have solitary heroes criticizing what most hold dear. We have breaks in the ranks on all sides—not only "flower children," but careful and rational adults. And not many of them are particularly heroic. This is evidence to me that there is a broadly based movement afoot. In the body of this study I described a process by which institutional authorities lost their moral force for some reasonable citizens of one neighborhood in Chicago. The process by which this happens throughout a nation must be similar in structure: institutionalized authorities fail to solve the moral problems of the era. Just look around.

So, there should be this movement away from taking traditional and official moral authorities seriously, and toward all those different destinations human complexity can devise. The measured experiments of interaction ritual are one such destination. But one thing is clear: there is no going back. It is impossible to re-create the conditions which made the traditions valid at one time. But it is possible to find a way to hang on to human essence in the epoch of cultural decline.

Victor Turner talks about the need to protect structure from antistructure. But this is a very relative matter, and when old value syntheses need reworking, antistructure is the only source of the new. Jürgen Habermas talks about the dynamics of "the rational society." His translator says:

> His thesis is that the structure [of communication] is free from constraint only when for all participants there is a symmetrical distribution of chances to select and employ speech acts, when there is an effective equality of chances to assume dialogue roles. In particular, all participants must have the same chance to initiate and perpetuate discourse, to put forward, call into question, and give reasons for or against statements, explanations, interpretations and justifications. Furthermore they must have the same chance to express attitudes, feelings, intentions and the like, and to command, to oppose, to permit and to forbid, etc.[4]

A society based on such communication has never been achieved, but Habermas argues that it is anticipated in every act of communication. No one in the Church of the Three Crosses, including myself, had even heard of Jürgen Habermas in 1971. But while he was articulating a theory in which free communication plays a central role, they were trying to practice it.

This is hardly a chance occurrence. The theory of Habermas and the practice of the Church of the Three Crosses are attempts to solve a problem of meaning which is peculiar to this culture, for the combination of Christianity, science, and large-scale organization has provided the West with the grandest system of moral certitude the world has ever known. As much as religion and science have fought each other, they have also worked together in practice. Science gave us reason to believe that we have reached the apex of human rationality. Christianity gave us reason to believe that we have *the* truth about man's ultimate destiny. These two systems, between them, have claimed to answer "all the questions" in an unprecedented way. And organizing made the answers effective. For decades the West has looked at all past cultures and all other cultures of the present world as predecessors or inferiors. What happened in Lincoln Park happened to ordinary heirs of this tradition.

---

[4] Thomas McCarthy, "Translator's Introduction" to *Legitimation Crisis*, by Jürgen Habermas (Boston: Beacon, 1975), p. *xvii.*

A culture which thought it had all the answers does not easily search for new ways to construct values. But if such is indeed the juncture at which we stand, then new ways of finding meaning must be devised. The options available in Lincoln Park in the late sixties may well represent the options available to Western culture itself.

Index

Index